Legacied

living

Lighter living

Declutter. Organize. Simplify.

Lisa J. Shultz

Lighter Living: Declutter. Organize. Simplify.
Published by High Country Publications
Breckenridge, Colorado
Copyright © 2019 by Lisa J. Shultz. All rights reserved.
www.LisaJShultz.com

FIRST EDITION
2019

Lighter Living: Declutter. Organize. Simplify.
Lisa J. Shultz

Names: Shultz, Lisa J., author.
Title: Lighter living : declutter. organize. simplify. / by Lisa J. Shultz.
Description: First trade paperback original edition. | Breckenridge [Colorado] :
High Country Publications, 2019. | Also published as an ebook.
Identifiers: ISBN 978-0-9986509-4-4
Subjects: LCSH: Storage in the home. | Orderliness. | House cleaning. | Com-
pulsive hoarding.
BISAC: SELF-HELP / Compulsive Behavior / Hoarding.
Classification: LCC TX321 | DDC 648.8–dc22

Library of Congress Control Number:2019914092

SELF-HELP / Personal Growth / Happiness

Book Design and Cover Design © 2019
Cover and Interior Design by Andrea Costantine
Editing by Bobby Haas
Author photo by PBMedia, LLC

All Rights Reserved by Lisa J. Shultz
and High Country Publications.

This book is printed in the United States of America.

For Summer and Liberty
and future generations

Contents

Introduction: Who Am I, and Where Did I Start?   1

    Why Read This Book?   4

    Is This Book About Minimalism?   6

    Ma   8

    Are There Different Kinds of Clutter?   9

    Is This Book a Fit For You?   11

    Respect and Apologies   12

    Additional Support   13

    Grab a Highlighter or Notebook   15

Chapter 1: Building a Case for Decluttering and Downsizing   17

    Family Chaos   21

    Sudden Death   22

    What is the Point of Decluttering My Life?   25

    Are There Stages of Decluttering?   31

    Empty Space   32

    What is Your Tipping Point?   33

Chapter 2: Digging In and Digging Out   37

    Schedule It   39

Hold It in Your Hands   42

In Search of the Superfluous   43

Clothes   46

Kitchen and Food Waste   48

Gifts   50

Catalogs, Magazines, and Books   52

Music   55

Papers   56

Garage   57

Chapter 3: Enrich or Ditch   59

Abandoned Hobbies, Sports Equipment,
   Pet Ashes, and the Potentially Useful   60

Sentimental and Historical Stuff   63

Chapter 4: Additional Considerations   77

Financial   77

Legal and Estate Documents   79

Social Media, Email, and Technology   80

Conversation   83

Sustainability and Environmental Impact   85

Carbon Footprint   90

Health   91

The Antiaging Movement   93

Internal Clutter   95

Feng Shui   96

Packing for Evacuation   97

Chapter 5: Lifelong Decluttering and Simplifying 99
    Progressive Downsizing 99
    Creating an Intentional Living Space 102
    When You Live with Someone Else 104
    Pets 105
    Aging in Place 106
    Energy 107
    Spirituality 109
    Unfinished Business 112

Final Thoughts: This Book Was Originally a Mess 115
    Wrapping Up 117
    A Millennial Perspective 119

Feedback 127
Endnotes, Books, Blogs, and Websites 129
Acknowledgments 139
About the Author 141

Who Am I, and Where Did I Start?

I am a baby boomer born in 1963. I live in the United States, splitting time between the city of Denver and the mountain town of Breckenridge, Colorado.

My parents got divorced in 1977, when I was a young teenager, and they never remarried. Each of them had spacious homes and both began filling up over time. When I married in 1988, my husband and I gradually went from a small condo to a medium-sized home and then to a very large house as his income grew. We blindly followed the trend that success was measured by buying a big house and lavishly decorating it. We filled all available space with material objects.

My marriage ended in 1999. The divorce was hard on me. I stayed in our overprovisioned house because I was exhausted from the upheaval of my marriage dissolving and single parenting. Despite feeling weighed down by the big house, I wanted the kids to have the stability of their home through their school years.

I didn't have much spare time to deal with all of the things our family had accumulated while my kids were growing up. Often, I stopped using items but never got rid of them. The stuff just stayed in closets, the basement, garage, or storage areas. The first book I read on the subject of clutter was in 2009, titled *Bless Your Mess* by Ashi, an acquaintance whom I had heard speak. Something clicked in my brain, and I realized that I had kept far too many things that the kids had outgrown. I scheduled a charity pick up, and my daughters and I started the process of thinning out our closets of unwanted clothing and toys.

I accelerated from basic decluttering to downsizing in 2012, when I sold my home after my youngest daughter graduated from high school. Our house was a three-story "mini mansion." In addition to a big kitchen, it contained five bedrooms, five bathrooms, four living/family rooms, two dining areas, an office, and a three-car garage. It was a 5,567-square-foot home. I moved to a new home with 1,836 square feet and no garage. I had to get rid of a lot of stuff before I could fit into the smaller space. But I cheated. I stored some items in my mom's garage and basement. The things I put there were items I had a hard time letting go of or ran out of time to deal with.

In 2015, my dad died, and I was largely responsible for emptying his house. When my mom's health was such that she needed to move into an assisted living facility, I had to disperse all of her stuff in 2018. Cleaning out two separate parental homes deeply affected me. Each house had an enormous amount of objects I had to personally handle. Then I had to do something with each one. My dad, in particular, felt everything was important and rarely threw anything away.

In the *Los Angeles Times* article "For Many People, Gathering Possessions is Just the Stuff of Life," author Mary MacVean wrote, "Consider these statistics cited by professional organizer Regina Lark: the average US household has 300,000 things, from paper clips to ironing boards."

Is it just me, or is that a ridiculous number of objects for one person, or even one family, to possess? Is there any wonder that I felt traumatized by the decision fatigue of dealing with each object in my big house before I downsized and then also cleared each of my parent's homes?

The good news is that I feel more benefits and fewer burdens since I decluttered, downsized, and narrowed down what is most important to me. Gradually, my priorities have shifted from being a consumer of things to a consumer of life. My home changed from a storage space to a sacred space. I began to feel less suffocated by stuff and now enjoy living a simplified life.

I am not a professional organizer or a counselor. I do not work in the mental health field. My original education and career was in physical therapy. However, I speak from experience because within the decade of 2009–2019, I downsized from my enormous home and cleared out both of my parent's houses. I felt like I was drowning in stuff when I added up all three houses. This book is a collection of my insights from, and candid reflections on, my journey of owning less.

Why Read This Book?

There are plenty of excellent books on the subject of clutter clearing, downsizing, and minimalism. I have read over twenty of them in the last decade, and each one pushed me a little further in the process of thinning out my belongings. I have not coined a new method, nor do I proclaim that I have it all done and figured out. I made discoveries as I distilled and assimilated books I read, and I wanted to share those discoveries in case they might provide additional insight and motivation. I integrated my experience as well. I offer personal examples of my life, but not as a suggestion that you must live just like me. Rather, I share stories and poke a little fun at myself to offset what otherwise might be a dry, preachy self-help book.

If you have had or anticipate a life transition, such as divorce or death of a loved one, children leaving the nest, or retirement, you may realize that you need to make some changes in where you live. Being a minimalist does not need to be your goal. But you may benefit from my book if you want to get rid of more stuff and need a spark to start or a nudge to carry on. You may experience self-empowerment when you take responsibility for reducing the amount of your stuff. And by taking control of your things, personal growth may extend to other parts of your life as well. This book will explore multiple benefits that decluttering may uncover; at the very least, you'll have a tidy home.

I cringe when I hear someone say, "I don't think my stuff is a problem, and I don't care what happens to it after I die." I urge people to be mindful and sensitive to those we leave behind upon our death. And we never know when our time will be up.

You may resonate more closely with this book if you have no children or your kids are grown or nearly so because I do not address the active child-raising phase. You might find yourself at the beginning, middle, or advanced stage in your simplification process. I still read books about decluttering to keep myself from stalling or regressing and to fortify myself from the temptations of buying more than I need. Feel free to test and experiment with my suggestions. Reject any that don't fit you. There is no one correct way. This book explores what happens when we tackle our stuff and decide what to do with it.

The benefits of lighter living are so broad and deep that they can't be boiled down to one end result. My hope is that you will find the process of consolidation to be satisfying and fulfilling. That was my experience. My choice of a lighter lifestyle has brought me a greater sense of well-being. In a world that often seems stressful and chaotic, that's a feeling I cherish.

Is This Book About Minimalism?

I use the term "minimalism" lightly in this book. You may be attracted or repelled by the word, considering it a craze or a phase. I consider minimalism not as a destination but rather as a tool and a mindset to reduce distractions and overwhelm. It is not a competition. You are a winner if you find the amount of stuff and size of your home to be perfect for you and your lifestyle and situation. You only lose if you never consider the potential benefits of decluttering and leave your loved ones with messes and burdens.

Those who first hear the word "minimalism" may think of a stark living environment, such as the well-known picture of the American business magnate Steve Jobs sitting on the floor in his living room in 1982.

Jobs was quoted as saying about the picture, "This was a very typical time. I was single. All you needed was a cup of tea, a light, and your stereo, you know, and that's what I had."

You may also envision monks or nuns living in sparsely decorated communes, or you may have read the book *Goodbye, Things: The New Japanese Minimalism* by Fumio Sasaki. The author gradually reduced his living space to a twenty-square-meter studio with a kitchen. He uses an air mattress on the floor to sleep.

Sasaki says, "I think it's time we started thinking about subtracting and refining to enhance the truly important things that might be buried deep down underneath all that excess."

Jobs and Sasaki are extreme examples of minimalism. You don't have to go that far. I have not gone that far. Avoid getting hung up on the word "minimalism." I am not suggesting that you reduce your possessions to a particular number or downsize to a certain square footage. The end result of minimizing does not mean you will live a spartan, sterile life with white, bare walls and a bed on the floor. I have art on my walls, decorate for the holidays, and have a few knickknacks. But I still consider myself progressing toward a minimalist lifestyle.

According to Joshua Becker, author and creator of BecomingMinimalist.com, "We were never meant to live life accumulating stuff. We were meant to live simply, enjoying the experiences of life, the people of life, and the journey of life—not the things of life." Becker describes minimalism as "the intentional promotion of the things we most value and the removal of everything that distracts from it. It is a highly personal journey that forces us to identify and articulate our highest values. Because of that, it is always going to be practiced differently by each individual." My home will look different from yours because we have different tastes and priorities. But ultimately, if we declutter our living spaces, we will be surrounded by what we use and love, and not much more. Becker boils the journey down to: "Own less stuff. Enjoy more freedom. It really is that simple."

Ma

If the word "minimalism" holds a negative charge for you, you may connect better with the concept of *ma*. According to Wikipedia, "*ma*" is a Japanese word which can be roughly translated as "gap," "space," "pause" or "the space between two structural parts." *Ma* has also been described as "an emptiness full of possibilities, like a promise yet to be fulfilled" and as "the silence between the notes that make the music."

My clearing has allowed me to rediscover things I stopped seeing and put them into a place of prominence. For me, if I allow *ma* into my home and my schedule, the stuff I own has space to be noticed, and furthermore, the activities I do are less hurried because they are not crammed together. I love to find places of honor for precious things, as well as savor the special events I attend.

As I embrace *ma*, I am more comfortable with empty space. Lauren Cassel Brownell wrote the book *Zen and the Art of Housekeeping: The Path to Finding Meaning in Your Cleaning*. She suggests, "We need to learn to see and understand the value of emptiness. If we can weed through some of the tangible barricades of possessions that we feel are protecting us—from loss, from loneliness, from something we cannot identify—we can begin to refill our empty spaces with what they really should be full of: love, laughter, creative pursuits, adventure, or perhaps just a little peace." What a great way to reframe the value of empty space!

Ma now guides my life, but of course, it was not always so. Previously, when invitations or opportunities to do something came my way, I attempted to squeeze in as many as possible. Now I focus on being less rushed and making the most of what I decide to do. And I relish in the space between my choices to rest and replenish myself. My new deliberate and slower pace has created a higher quality in my experiences.

Are There Different Kinds of Clutter?

Perhaps you are ready to look at the multidimensional ways that clutter can manifest itself in your life.

- Physically: cleaning, moving, storing, managing
- Mentally: stressing, distracting, overwhelming
- Emotionally: apathy, sadness, anger, fear
- Spiritually: dulling, clogging, disconnection

You will read about all these different aspects later in the book, and they are often intertwined with each other. The things that surround us in our lives can affect physical and mental health. The clearing process can be cathartic and healing. Sometimes we may cling to stuff in fear. Clutter may rob us of the life we imagined or prevent us from creating a new vision for our future.

When I first started to get rid of things in my house, and then in the homes of both of my parents, I went through phases in how the process affected me. At first, I enjoyed a bit of clearing. But after a while, I felt burdened and angry. I asked myself why I had bought all of this stuff in the first place. Why had my parents not dealt with their things themselves? When the process became a full-time job, I felt depleted and mildly depressed. I could not believe that my parents and I had so many physical objects. How much does one person need? I felt that days, weeks, months, and years of my life were wasted by the removal of stuff. There were more important things I would rather have been doing. But I continued, and eventually, I felt lighter and freer than I had ever felt in the years of big houses with each room filled to the brim.

I started to view every space in my home differently. If the space wasn't used, it was not worth having. I felt the need to downsize further and determine what my "senior home" might look like and whether or not it was a good place to age. Being the daughter who dealt with eldercare and wrapping up the affairs of my parents had a sobering effect on my vision for my future. Losing the buffer zone of my parents meant I was next. I had a chance to craft a lighter finale for my future senior years. I didn't want the final chapters of my life to be about stuff, and I didn't want to abandon the responsibility of dealing with it myself. Instead, I desired more time for relationships and experiences with friends and family. I wanted to break free from the ball and chain of too much stuff. I desired peace of mind that would allow me to dig deeper into a purposeful life without regrets.

Is This Book a Fit For You?

If you are just starting your journey in ridding yourself of unneeded things, I can offer some tips in getting started. I have recommendations to guide you through breaking the shopping habit and how to sort and disperse your possessions. I also offer suggestions for organizing your affairs and the stuff you keep. This book is also geared toward the intermediate. You may have already downsized your home and gotten rid of a substantial amount of possessions, but then you stopped. You might want a kick in the pants to get going again but need more reasons why you should carve out the time to do so. You might need persuasion as to why it makes sense to dig deeper into getting rid of additional stuff.

Think of my book like a recipe for chocolate cake. It is just one of many recipes, not necessarily the best one. You can decide to try the recipe, but more likely, you will pick ingredients to put into your own recipe. Your age and stage of life may not be the same as mine. You may live with someone. You may have constraints that you have to work around. There is no contest in this minimalistic direction, and I don't judge those with bigger homes and more possessions: It is not my business. You have my permission to select parts you like and forget about the rest. In the end, you will have the perfect chocolate cake for yourself.

Respect and Apologies

I respect and credit other minimizers and authors who published before me. There are many good books, blogs, and websites for you to browse if you choose. I enjoy quoting those immersed in this shared passion. Each has unique experiences and niches you might want to check out. We are all in this exploration together; it is not a competition. I hope I have accurately quoted and credited others. In the back of this book, I list notes with references for you to tap into as you dig deeper.

I would like to apologize to family members and friends who were the recipients of things I was getting rid of in my massive decluttering phase. I hope that you have kept only those things you love and use and have gotten rid of the rest.

I love my parents deeply and am grateful for all they provided me. I acknowledge and respect that I do not know what it was like to have grown up during the Great Depression and lived through World War II. Those influences spilled into my boomer generation and beyond, and I am trying to break free of the parts that aren't helpful for me today. In the past, scarcity due to rationing may have elicited a keep-everything mindset, but perhaps now you might find that holding onto things in case they could be used in some way may not be as necessary.

I honor the generations into which my parents were born. My mom and dad were remarkable people. I admire and appreciate them for many reasons. This book is really not about them; it is about me. They never intended to burden me with clearing out their homes. I suspect they became almost paralyzed by the quantity of their possessions, and then disability or death made it impossible for them to take personal action. Plus, my dad, in particular, was sentimental and saw value in everything. So the job got left to someone else. I forgive them.

I decided to break the trend of accumulating stuff sooner rather than later. I moved to smaller homes ahead of my need. I downsized before I was forced to do so. I sorted and dispersed my things while I had the energy and the ability to either donate or sell my stuff. I am still in middle age, but as an aging boomer, time marches on and seems to rush by faster each year. I am no longer young, but I am not yet old. In many ways, I am in the prime of my life. I have enough stuff and don't want unloved and unused things to hold me down from enjoying the perks of middle age. Raising children and caregiving for my parents is now behind me. It is a special time for me. It is my moment to savor, relish, and celebrate—but with experiences rather than material things.

If you are open to divesting the volume of your belongings, let's continue.

Additional Support

When I dug deeper in clearing stuff, I found buried emotions and unprocessed loss. If this happens to you, additional support might be in order. Decluttering can be done alone, but it is okay to seek support.

I like taking yoga classes while I am releasing objects and emotions that are no longer helpful in my present-day life. Bodies can hold emotional baggage too. I have heard yogis use the term "emotional junk drawer." Hips are often spots people store emotions. In her article for *Yoga Today* titled "Hips Don't Lie: Releasing Old Emotions Through Hip Openers," Megan McIntruff explains, "Whether it is one traumatic event, or multiple small events, the feelings of fear, anxiety, and sadness are stored at the hips until we bring them to the surface and allow a release. The longer you suppress emotion, the tighter the grasp."

I found yoga helpful to loosen up my hips and other areas of my body where I carry tension—tension I could experience in the decluttering process. In the process of decluttering things in my life, I was peeling off the layers of my past that no longer mattered to my present life. But as I did that shedding, memories and emotions arose. I sometimes felt sadness as I removed reminders of a failed marriage or the loss of a loved one. I grieved lost dreams and deceased people and pets. If I looked for it, I also experienced gratitude for the good times and the love that once was. Eventually, I felt lighter after I worked my way through a particular emotional zone that exposed remnants of unhealed parts of my life.

Along with yoga for wellness and release of stuck energy, I also incorporate acupuncture. My acupuncturist can detect and clear areas of my body where energy is stagnant. If an organ system is working too hard or is weak, she creates treatment to strengthen it or settle it down. Meditation helps calm my mind when I am stuck in rumination or worry. Stress affects each person differently, and a skilled acupuncturist, healing practitioner, or meditation practice can guide the body back to balance, curb a wandering mind, and promote healing.

Hiring a professional therapist or coach might be in order as well. Asking a friend or family member to be with you while you deal with a particularly difficult part of your home or stored belongings may be helpful. Taking a course or class might bring you together with others who have similar goals. There are groups called Clutterers Anonymous that go through a twelve-step program together. You do not need to take this journey alone. Gather support as needed.

Grab a Highlighter or Notebook

Before you continue reading, grab a highlighter or notebook to mark up or write down what parts of this book resonate with you. At the end, I would like to hear from you. I may write a blog with more information and additional resources that my readers share with me.

Here we go!

CHAPTER ONE

Building a Case for Decluttering and Downsizing

For my parents and me, clutter insidiously crept in on us slowly over time. We just didn't give it much thought. We were busy with family life, working, and many responsibilities and activities.

I started to become more aware and sensitive to stress, particularly after my divorce. When I no longer had a marital partner to share responsibilities of taking care of a large home, it might have behooved me to move into a smaller place. But I was daunted by the decision and the process involved in finding a new house and moving by myself with two little children.

The major shift in our family dynamic clouded the feeling of my home as an oasis. The house felt heavier to me as I managed it alone. Each year that passed in the big house drained my bank account because there was always something to fix or maintain. Peter Walsh wrote the book *It's All Too Much*, and in it, he said, "Your home should be the antidote to stress—not the cause of it." Since I didn't move until many years later, I didn't have the chance to simplify as soon as it might have been optimal. It was hard for me to take care of that big house, and consequently, there were plenty of spaces where clutter accumulated.

Then there is the harsh reality of aging and death. We may avoid thinking about either, or both, due to fear. Losing our parents has the potential to bring increased awareness of the natural cycle of life. Margareta Magnusson provided a reality check in her book *The Gentle Art of Swedish Death Cleaning: How to Free Yourself and Your Family from a Lifetime of Clutter.* Magnusson says, "Aging is certainly not for weaklings. That is why you should never wait too long to start your downsizing. Sooner or later, you will have your own infirmities, and then it is damn nice to be able to enjoy the things you can still manage to do without the burden of too many things to look after and too many messes to organize." I was able to embrace this downsizing suggestion in my late forties and fifties. And I have no regrets other than I could have saved a lot of money if I had done it sooner.

Magnusson also addresses leaving a burden to others. "Do not ever imagine that anyone will wish—or be able—to schedule time off to take care of what you didn't bother to take care of yourself. No matter how much they love you, don't leave this burden to them." As I cleaned out all the stuff in my parents' homes, I had to process resentment, anger, and stress at a time of grief. Adding those additional emotions can further complicate mourning and even leave you feeling robbed of fully appreciating the experience.

I have deep compassion for my dad. Aging was really hard for him. He was accustomed to being a vibrant and successful man, and each loss of ability or mobility hurt him deeply. Retaining his possessions provided him comfort. His things were full of history and stories and were part of his identity. I suspect that keeping all his stuff helped offset his age-related losses. His things might have insulated him from the fear of his inevitable disappearance from his earthly existence. It was difficult for him to conceive of his death or the loss of material objects. He was challenged with letting go of life and things. I suspect he held on tightly because he hated losing control and enjoyed his life before disability set in.

For example, my dad loved his collection of Native American artifacts and cowboy paraphernalia. His living room was like a museum, which was really cool to visit, but nothing in that collection fit my personality or lifestyle. Fortunately, one of my brothers took a large part of it, but sometimes, no one in the family wants their parents' collections. Magnusson talks about our beloved treasures. "You can always hope and wait for someone to want something in your home, but you cannot wait forever, and sometimes you must just give cherished things away with the wish that they end up with someone who will create new memories of their own."

When I sold my big house, there was no room for the family pool table in my smaller space. It had been my grandfather's and then my dad's. It was brought from South Dakota to Colorado and was in my childhood home and then my home as an adult. I agonized about that table as I prepared to sell my house. Eventually, I put the word out to friends to see if someone wanted it. A friend of a friend spoke up and took it into his home. He assured me that it would be well used and loved by his family. I rarely played pool, and it had been gathering dust in my house. Now it would be a focal point of enjoyment again. It had gone to strangers, but it eased my mind to deliver it into function and fun for others.

Despite the harsh reality of our final years of life, joy can be found. Magnusson states, "Death cleaning is also something you can do for yourself, for your own pleasure. And if you start early, at say sixty-five, it won't seem like such a huge task when you, like me, are between eighty and 100. One's own pleasure, and the chance to find meaning and memory, is the most important thing. It is a delight to go through things and remember their worth. And if you don't remember why a thing has meaning or why you kept it, it has no worth, and it will be easier for you to part with."

I didn't wait until sixty-five, and I am glad. Things I found of worth during my physical therapy career, in my active child-raising years, competitive sports period, or during my marriage all felt dated and no longer purposeful. Surrounding myself, instead, with my current interests and tastes felt exhilarating.

Finally, it might behoove us to envision the scene of our home after we die. Who do you want to profit from your things? *The Gentle Art of Swedish Death Cleaning* paints a picture. "If you cannot find anyone to give your possessions to, sell them and make a donation to charity. If you don't death clean and show people what is valuable, once you die, there will be a big truck that takes all the wonderful things you have to an auction (at best) or a dump. No one will be happy about that. Well, the auction house might be." If you would rather not visualize a dumpster outside your house after you die, you still have time to do something about it.

Family Chaos

I was lucky. My siblings and I were harmonious in the process of clearing out our parents' homes. Julie Hall, The Estate Lady®, wrote the book *The Boomer Burden: Dealing with your Parents' Lifetime Accumulation of Stuff.* In her experience she explains "Fewer than 20 percent of the estates I've handled have gone smoothly. The rest have been filled with confusion, anger, jealousy, huge legal expenses, and broken relationships between siblings."

Hall warns you might be feeling dread: "You see your parents becoming more afflicted with age and fragility, and you are hit by a dizzying feeling of all the details about to land in your lap. I call this experience "the flying brick," and it will strike you right between the eyes if you are not prepared … Being in denial will help no one, least of all your parents. Don't wait to deal with these issues until a moment of crisis, or that flying brick will turn into a boulder."

I am incredibly grateful for my siblings' and my ability to reason and support the decision to sell parental homes and clear them without acrimony. But I can relate to Hall's dismal statistics on the likelihood of dispute at the end of a parent's life, in regard to their homes or possessions. I regularly get together with some childhood friends for support and hear their horror stories of conflict. No matter what stage you are in, acknowledging that our possessions, homes, and affairs can be problematic to those we leave behind is the first step toward taking proactive measures to reduce potential chaos and strife among those destined to deal with it.

Sudden Death

In my local mountain newspaper, the *Summit Daily News*, I read in December of 2018 a story entitled: "Family remembers Arvada man who died following cardiac event at Keystone." The picture shows a smiling man on the ski slopes, age fifty-two. He was three years younger than

I was at the time, which caught my eye. His first cardiac event killed him without warning.

The article provided the man's background and a glimpse of his personality and passions. He had two kids, ages twenty-three and twenty-one, who were struggling to deal with his loss on many levels. I enjoyed reading about his life until I got to the point where it was revealed that he had not done any planning for the inevitable—his ultimate death. I then felt heartsick for his kids, who are just a bit younger than mine. The article quoted his daughter: "This was his first cardiac event, so I don't think even *he* was prepared for it. There's no will, no life insurance, and no financial records … so we have nothing, and we're the only people our dad had."

The article then went on to say that the family was still hoping to find the man's financial records or a will on his computer but had not been able to gain access because no passwords were left. The family started a Go-FundMe campaign to help raise money for his funeral service. I cringed in anguish for his children. I gathered that they were a close family, but the kids had no road map on how to settle their father's affairs or even how to pay for his funeral. Most likely, they had to hire an attorney and go through probate and spent most of the following year dealing with legal matters on top of the grief and emotional pain of losing their dad. That story is an important reminder that we may not live into old age and getting our affairs in order now is prudent. Furthermore, we could also unexpectedly be incapacitated or disabled. We would not want a crisis situation to be compounded by guesses about our wishes. As we tidy our homes, we can organize our paperwork and legal documents too.

Perhaps you are not moved by the woes of cleaning out parental houses or concerned about the possibility of unexpected death. Maybe you are still searching for a compelling reason to consider decluttering or downsizing. It is possible that you don't even have that much stuff but are looking for tips on reducing overwhelm and increasing focus in your life. You may feel like you are at the mercy of your job and that you are not able to design your own life. You may also realize that you are easily swayed by savvy marketing and want to take charge of your spending habits. Perhaps debt reduction is becoming an increasing priority, as well as saving for retirement. I believe that no matter what situation in life you find yourself, there is room for you to take control of little things, which ultimately adds up to big things. And self-initiated decluttering is a baby step in the big picture of your ultimate objective.

Stuff can both paralyze and control you. Our mindset can work for us or against us. I relate to the scenario of sunk-cost bias, which Greg McKeown explains in his book *Essentialism: The Disciplined Pursuit of Less.* "Sunk-cost bias is the tendency to continue to invest time, money, or energy into something we know is a losing proposition simply because we have already incurred, or sunk, a cost that cannot be recouped. But, of course, this can easily become a vicious cycle: The more we invest, the more determined we become to see it through and see our investment pay off. The more we invest in something, the harder it is to let go."

Might your house, your job, or a project apply to that bias? McKeown goes on to say, "An essentialist has the courage and confidence to admit his or her mistakes and uncommit, no matter the sunk costs." It takes gumption to change directions when you discover a sunk-cost bias, but ultimately, it may be in your best interest to do so.

What is the Point of Decluttering My Life?

If you are beginning to simplify your life or you need encouragement to keep moving in that direction, reconnect to your deepest values. It is possible that our complex world has taken you farther away instead of closer to what you cherish most. Courtney Carver is the author of the book *Soulful Simplicity*. She says, "Start to think about what really matters to you. If you aren't sure at first, don't worry. Sometimes you have to get rid of the things that don't matter to let the things that do rise to the surface."

Perhaps you crave deeper relationships. You may want to travel or spend more time in nature. But if your life and home have become full of too many activities and things to take care of and bills to pay, then restructuring might be in order. In the last decade, I have been peeling off parts of my life that had become distractors from what makes my heart feel peaceful and fulfilled. I have downsized my home, sold businesses, and gotten good at saying, "No, thank you." I also looked at every bill that came my way and every expense I was paying. Carver says, "I finally figured it out. Instead of working so hard to make ends meet, work on having fewer ends."

I practiced restraint and took control of my expenditures. I thought about necessities: I paid utility and maintenance bills for my house, maintained my car, and bought food. I also value health and wellness, so I continued to see healthcare practitioners and spent money on yoga, dance, sports, and exercise classes. But shopping for anything else was eliminated. I restricted inflow because I had enough stuff. I did not allow myself to be tempted with shiny objects such as new phones, computers, and electronic gadgets. I only purchased something new when my current one died and could not be repaired. Hence, I drive an old car with over 200,000 miles on it, my laptop is almost a decade old, and my phone has a cracked screen but works fine. I do not need the latest and greatest advances in technology. I will eventually have it, but only when the device or vehicle I currently have no longer functions.

My voluntary simplicity might also be called "frugal," and I am okay with that. But I don't live a life of deprivation. Money saved by avoidance of unnecessary spending provides money for things that really mean something to me and for my retirement fund. Professional organizer and author Peter Walsh believes, "You only have one life to live. How you live that life is your choice. As far as I know, no one has ever inscribed 'I wish I had bought more stuff' on their tombstone. What you own can easily blind you to who you are and what you can be."

I feel more room for writing creatively when I reduce busyness. When I own less, fewer things go wrong and need to be fixed. I have more space: openings in my calendar, room in my home, and calm in my heart. I also like to plan special vacations. I love being able to say yes to adventure and opportunities that will add meaning and deep fulfillment to my life. When I am stretched thin with too many responsibilities and obligations, my focus is scattered. I wallow in overwhelm and waste time on trivial matters.

The questions of "Who am I?" and "Why am I here?" have been asked for a long time. Perhaps you have a handle on those questions and devote yourself to a mission, passion, or livelihood that brings meaning to your life. Maybe you are becoming a master at an art or profession. You might be immersed in a cause that helps humanity and our planet. But you could also be drifting and lost, looking for temporary fixes to satiate longings because you don't know who you are and what the point of life is for you. Could it be that clutter clogs our path toward understanding ourselves? Carver states, "Getting rid of everything that doesn't matter allows you to remember who you are. Simplicity doesn't change who you are; it brings you back to who you are." As I declutter and downsize, I gradually discover more of my essence and my purpose.

The idea of the self behind the stuff fascinates me. I resonated with a passage in the book *Breathing Room* by Lauren Rosenfeld and Dr. Melva Green: "Your possessions are not you. If all of your possessions were to vanish, you would still be you. You would still be whole. You would still have a history. You would still love what you love … you came into this world with nothing. You'll leave with nothing. In the period in between, you will amass possessions and stories and emotions around your possessions. Some of these possessions, emotions, and stories serve you, while others do not. But none of it … is actually you."

If this notion of who you really are feels vague, perhaps you are curious how your life would look and feel without so much stuff surrounding you. Who might you become with the growth that happens when you contemplate your purpose within this life? How will you feel when you drop stories, barriers, and material things that hold you back from living your best life now? Do you have a vision of what a freer life might look like? Ponder these and similar questions, consider some answers, and invariably, you will grow.

In Alan Arkin's book *Out of My Mind*, he talks about growth. "Growth is often at first accompanied by sadness and melancholy. It is almost always at first accompanied by a sense of loss, of giving up something, losing something … Internal growth is almost always a pairing away, shedding, getting rid of rather than accumulating. Invariably what I have lost is some fantasy version of myself and the world, not the way I would have designed things, but no one asked me. It takes time for growth to feel good and right and strong, but eventually it does."

My efforts at clearing my clutter did not always feel blissful while I was in the middle of it. Growth was not always immediate. When I dug into a box containing my wedding keepsakes, for example, I felt grief. I didn't pretend to myself that the loss of that dream was insignificant. Thirty years after my wedding, I unwrapped engraved champagne classes from tissue paper and held them in my hands—one with my name on it and one with his. I let the emotions and memories surface and flow through me. Knowing my daughters didn't want them and allowing that memory to play out in my mind and my heart enabled me to put the glasses into the recycle bin in peace.

Would it have been better if I had taken those glasses and disposed of them at the time of my divorce? I do not know because I did not do that. I wasn't ready to say goodbye to them at that time. But I believe that I should not have waited thirty years to clear out that box. The problem was that I put that box in the basement and forgot about it. And it wasn't in my own basement; it was my mom's basement! So when I cleaned out her home, I found pockets of my own stuff to deal with during that already difficult time. I don't advocate storing things in anyone else's home or renting a storage space. I suggest taking care of it sooner rather than later. Processing loss and grief is an important part of healing. Each time I have allotted time to dig into it instead of storing it for later, I have experienced additional heart healing. That box of wedding mementos represented my past, not my present life. Releasing its contents opened up my heart and paved the way for what I wanted in my life now and in the future.

Uncovering existential meaning beneath your things or finding purpose or direction in your life may not resonate with you as a reason to declutter. Perhaps you click with the concept of *ma*, where the things that are meaningful to you pop visually in your home. Or maybe you are tired of the weight of the stuff you have amassed. Once you break away from the heaviness of clutter, you may feel lighter. Francine Jay, known as Miss Minimalist, wrote *The Joy of Less*. In it, she says, "When we're no longer chained to our stuff, we can savor life, connect with others, and participate in our communities. We're more open to experiences and better able to recognize and take advantage of opportunities. The less baggage we're dragging around (both physically and mentally), the more living we can do!"

Are There Stages of Decluttering?

Journeys often have stages, but they are dynamic and can repeat or be slightly different due to your unique situation and personality. These are the stages I found myself experiencing while decluttering and downsizing:

1. Contemplating decluttering—I am becoming aware of benefits.
2. Motivation and enthusiasm—I am ready!
3. Starting and digging in—I overcame inertia, and I am immersed in the process of clearing.
4. Overwhelm and frustration—I didn't know it would be this hard!
5. Anger—Why did I (or my parents) buy and/or keep all this stuff?
6. Stalled—Maybe I can't do this job.
7. Resolve and recommitment—I will keep going!
8. Over the hump—I can see a finish line of a project or move!
9. Experiencing benefits—I continue decluttering because that burden feeling of being weighed down is lifting and is being replaced by lightness.
10. Maintenance of less stuff—I tidy up regularly and am a good gatekeeper. I am developing a new normal and avoiding the relapse of old behaviors.

Empty Space

When I eventually moved to a smaller home, it felt cozy, like having a pair of jeans that fit me just right—no wasted living space and no baggy fabric. It felt wonderful! I love having a great room that contains my kitchen, dining room, and living room as one large space. Decluttering each part of my home made it feel bigger and allowed me breathing room despite less square footage. Avoid feeling claustrophobic, like wearing pants that are binding at your waist, when considering a smaller living space. By looking at and perhaps temporarily living in a smaller home, you may find a size that will feel perfect for you.

This declutter and downsize direction is more than physical objects and the size of your home. I have given several examples of how my mind and my emotions are closely tied to it all. I made the decision to prioritize the process. That choice required that I carve out time in my schedule or drop activities that kept me too busy to deal with it. Perhaps I crammed my calendar full to cover up loneliness and emptiness. Other people might fill that void with alcohol, drugs, food, shopping, and a plethora of other coping methods. We humans often feel ill-equipped to allow space and silence into our lives. We can be uncomfortable with the idea of *ma*. I asked myself, "Who would I be if I weren't busy? What would be left of my life and of me after I removed excess stuff from my home and allowed my day to have unscheduled open spaces?"

I cannot tell you who you will become without so many things surrounding you. But I can say that I was pleased with the discoveries I made, and I will attempt to share a few with you in the pages ahead. I didn't need to fear the process. It was full of treasure. And that treasure is available to all of us.

What is Your Tipping Point?

If you are just starting your process of getting rid of things, something must have prompted you to do so. For me, I had a gradual awakening that I owned too much stuff in 2009 when I read the book *Bless Your Mess.* But the tipping point that catapulted me to further downsize and declutter was finding myself responsible for clearing two parental homes. I spent a considerable chunk of time in 2015 and 2018 handling each object my parents owned, making a decision about it, and then implementing that decision. It took months of physical labor, mental energy, and emotional stress. I had to set aside my own routine and activities. At the same time, I had to curb my resentment over spending my valuable time getting rid of someone else's lifetime collections of stuff. It forced me to view my own full house with the potential of handing the same burden to my daughters. It all felt heavy, and I wanted to feel lighter.

I began my own journey to feeling lighter by defining what benefits I hoped to experience. The first step on the path of a decluttering journey is finding your why. Here is a list of reasons to declutter that might apply to you.

- Financially overextended
- Desire for debt reduction
- Need to increase retirement funds and savings
- Want to break a compulsion to shop and buy unnecessary items
- Wish to eliminate impulse buying and substitute intentional buying
- Concerned about our society's propensity for overconsumption
- Disillusionment with materialism
- Home bigger than you need
- More things than you need
- Life situation change: divorce, death, kids move out
- Wish to not burden your family if you become disabled and when you die
- Health issues
- Aging considerations—living independently as a senior
- Environmental consciousness and desire to lessen negative impact on the planet
- Disconnection, disillusion, dissatisfaction
- Overwhelm, anxiety, stress, depression
- Want more time, energy, freedom
- Desire to give more

- Fed up with trivial distractions and disorder
- Wish to increase purposeful focus
- Freedom to play or travel more and pursue dreams

Once you are clear about your motivation for making changes and are ready to begin, take a deep breath and take one action step today. Clean out the easiest spot you can think of, something with no emotional attachment or negative association. Perhaps you clear your refrigerator of old and expired food items or remove worn out socks or underwear from your dresser drawer. If you live with someone, focus on your own things. Be careful not to remove your partner's or another family member's belongings without permission.

Next, get connected to others who are on the same journey. This may or may not be a person you are living with currently. They may not be ready for the changes you seek, but eventually, watching your progress may influence them. I suggest reading additional books and blogs about clutter clearing or minimalism. See the back of this book for a resource list.

You may be in a hurry to change your situation, or you may need to take it slowly. It is not a race, and the speed of the journey is not important. Continue until you feel lighter and have achieved some of your goals. You may do that in a year or ten. I will be here to cheer you on, no matter how long it takes.

Let's continue with how to sort and clear your living spaces.

CHAPTER TWO

Digging In and Digging Out

We just went through a lot of reasons you might want to consider or continue decluttering. Without that solid foundation to justify this work, you are unlikely to progress through all the stages.

In my reading, I have found different approaches to dealing with clutter. I have tried most all of them. I didn't find one that was the magic formula, nor am I presenting you with a new strategy. But I have suggestions.

"Confront the difficult while it is still easy;
accomplish the great task by a series of small acts."
—Tao Te Ching

Decluttering and downsizing can be laborious. But if taken baby step by baby step, it can be done. My first suggestion is to think of decluttering in little chunks of time, even thirty minutes here and there. Set a timer and clear one space each day or each week and repeat consistently.

You may also want to consider removing items you keep at someone else's house or a storage unit. Unless there is some special, temporary reason for it, perhaps deal with those items first. It doesn't get easier later and may even be worse. I found myself with unnecessary extra stress when I had to clear my mom's house prior to selling it and also deal with my things in her basement and garage as well. Delaying the task of eliminating my storage items compounded over time.

Within your own home, I suggest waiting on sentimental possessions and photographs for last, or you might get stuck. Start with parts of your house that are not daunting, tossing pure junk, and gather momentum from there. Declutter in small steps and with the easiest things first to build confidence. Clear items from room to room or pick a category. My decision-making motto is to ask myself if the item benefits me or burdens me. Does an object have a purpose? Do I use it? Is it meaningful or beautiful? If the answer is yes, it benefits me, then it can stay through my first round of clearing.

For each round of decluttering, I have bags or boxes for the following categories:

- Relocate
- Recycle

- Donate
- Sell
- Trash

I am a big fan of recycling and donating things before dumping them into a landfill. But I realize some things are pure junk and need to be tossed into the garbage bin.

Schedule It

If you tend to use the "I'm too busy" excuse for not clearing your clutter, schedule it. Stephen Covey claims, "The key is not to prioritize what's on your schedule, but to schedule your priorities." You can pick a day, a weekend, or if you are really motivated, carve out a whole week or more. Perhaps you need to take it slowly, or maybe you want to work at a fast pace. I have successfully used both methods. One time, I cleaned and cleared every Tuesday for months. Another time, I paused everything I was doing and reserved a week for a major clear. To make your time productive and efficient, there is some necessary prep work.

- Collect boxes, trash bags, and tissue or newspaper if you have fragile items to move.
- Alert anyone who has stuff stored at your house and give them a deadline for removal.
- Return any items you borrowed from someone else.

- Relocate things to the room where they belong.
- Research charities and donation centers: get hours, locations, and rules.
- Research online sale options: establish accounts and investigate what prices similar items are selling for.
- Visit consignment stores and set up appointments to review your items.
- Ask friends for assistance: lifting and carrying, hauling things to donation centers, helping with a yard sale.
- Round up everything that is broken or needs to be fixed. Either take it to a repair shop or use superglue or duct tape or find tools and attempt to repair it yourself. If unsuccessful, dispose of it.
- Toss dead or dying plants; trim the keepers as needed.
- Begin gathering any stuff you have not used in a year, as well as any duplicates.
- Establish a room or space to place all supplies and the gathering mound of things that are being donated or might be candidates for selling.

Giving things to those in need gave me satisfaction. I highly recommend researching agencies and groups that will welcome items you no longer need, use, or love. If you decide to sell your things, beware of the trap of thinking your stuff has more value than it really has. Just because you spent a lot of money on it or someone told you it was worth something does not mean it has value. You may feel like you are wasting your money selling something for a low price or giving it to charity. Wanting instant gratification or desiring retail therapy is common in our culture. But if you are establishing a higher priority of breathing room and peace of mind, forgive yourself for past purchases. Move forward to a healthier mindset and let go of needing to recoup your money.

Selling can be a time-consuming hassle. Nonetheless, I did sell some items in my process of downsizing. Occasionally, that made me feel a bit better, offsetting the irritation I had for buying so much in the first place. I also recommend selling things if you have debt. Take your earnings and pay down loans or money you owe others.

When I designed a purge week, I had a method. On the weekend prior to the designated week, I posted items for sale on Craigslist and other online platforms. Each day, I checked the listings and reduced the price incrementally. On the last weekend of my purge, if something had not sold, I either posted the item as free, placed it in a garage sale, drove it to a donation center, or arranged pick up from a charity that accepted such items.

During the days of this purge week, I went room to room and looked at everything with discerning eyes. Often, I thought of someone who might find something useful, so I called them and inquired if they wanted it. I am not a fan of garage sales because when I had one, I thought it was a ton of work without much money to show for it. But if you want to have one, ask someone who has experience and success with them to help you. You can also Google "How to have a successful garage sale" for multiple resources and ideas. I made a lot of mistakes, due to being clueless about how to run one effectively.

Purge weeks are particularly efficient prior to a move. Designating and prioritizing a day of the week consistently for several months can make a big, positive difference. You may want to consider a room or zone per month if you are spreading out your clearing process over a longer period of time. It is also a good idea to give yourself a deadline, such as completing a project or section of your home by your next birthday or the end of the summer or end of the year.

Hold It in Your Hands

Marie Kondo wrote the books *The Life Changing Magic of Tidying Up* and *Spark Joy*. She also has a blog and Netflix show on tidying up. She advocates holding each item you own in your hands and asking yourself, "Does this spark joy?" If it does, keep it. If not, dispose of it." The word "joy" didn't always work for me, so I have substituted "benefit" or "burden" as I touch everything I own.

Your body can be a reliable compass if you tap into it. If you hold an object in your hands and sit with it, you will begin to feel the energy of it. You will sense if it should stay or go. On occasion, you may be uncertain, and that is okay. You can create a holding spot for items that need to be reevaluated later. Like peeling an onion, it is best to take it one layer at a time. This is also another reason to declutter over a period of time: doing so allows you to revisit items rather than feeling forced to make a decision on the spot. If you have avoided dealing with an excess of stuff in your life, you may have other incomplete and unfinished business in your life as well. Later, we will discuss deeper psychological components that might be holding you back from releasing some of your things. For now, take items without emotional charges associated with them and handle each one of them, one at a time. Choosing words like "joy" or "benefit" or "burden" to describe how you viscerally feel about an item might help you determine whether or not to keep or dispose of it.

In Search of the Superfluous

I love the word "superfluous." It is an adjective, and according to dictionary.com, it means "being more than is sufficient or required; excessive." It also means "unnecessary or needless." But wait, there is more! It also means: "obsolete, possessing or spending more than enough or necessary; extravagant."

When I considered this word in the context of decluttering, I began to use it in many ways. I walked around my home opening every cabinet, cupboard, drawer, closet, and box. I evaluated the contents of every nook and cranny in my house in search of the superfluous. It was everywhere. How many office supplies do I need? How many duplicate kitchen items do I have? How many spare linens and towels do I require? Looking for extras and consolidating multiples—that is, looking for the superfluous—is a terrific place to start decluttering.

I began to place the superfluous items into donation bags or boxes. As my house became less cluttered, I was better able to see what I owned and find things with ease. I was also supporting those in need with items they could use.

I also guarded my pocketbook to reduce or eliminate any redundant purchases. Other than a few extra rolls of toilet paper and key items that I go through rapidly, I ceased stockpiling or searching for bargains. I much prefer the clean look of shelves with open spaces than those crammed with objects. I also quit accepting promotional giveaways, swag, and freebies.

The vigilance of superfluous became a mantra and a habit. It became part of my everyday mentality. If I had a spare minute here or there, I would revisit a section of my home to double-check any previous clearing. I always found pockets that I had neglected before because they contained sentimental items or things I thought I might need someday. When I find one of those pockets that I want to clear but feel hesitant, I often set the things out onto a table that I walk by frequently. I just let them sit there for a day. I am giving that stuff a chance to make an appeal, convince me I really need it in my life.

After a day of questionable items bugging me by clogging space on a vital area like my dining table, I find it easier to take the next step of finding a new home for them. But if I am still not ready to let a thing go, I might try a one-month test. (I put an item in a box, and if I don't pull it out to use it in the next four weeks, I get rid of it.) An exception might be seasonal items, but if I don't use them during that time of year, I move them out as well.

While decluttering, sometimes I had to process the loss of a dream. I may have had to relinquish the hope I had for a goal. I looked at items associated with my active versus defunct hobbies and made a realistic decision about the likelihood of resurrecting those abandoned hobbies again. In some cases, I also needed time to find a new home for something to help me to feel better. If I chose a place or a person who might cherish the thing or things, it eased my mind a bit. I often photographed an item to remember it or show it to someone else. Accepting that an era of my life was over or a relationship had dissolved, or forgiving someone or myself required time and a willingness to look deeper within my heart.

At first glance, the search and removal of the superfluous seemed like a housekeeping or organizing task. In reality, it led me to inner work and reflection. And although it was a difficult process at times, I am glad I took the time and energy to evaluate my stuff and my motives for having it. I am responsible for what I have gathered in my life and what to do about it. And in a way, it never ends, but it does get easier. At least that has been my experience thus far.

Clothes

Marie Kondo suggests tidying by category, not location. She says to begin with clothes, which can be found in multiple rooms or closets throughout the home. We usually wear 20 percent of our clothes 80 percent of the time. I suggest ceasing to buy new clothes while clearing. Take every single piece of clothing out of every drawer, box, closet—anywhere in the entire house—and sort: consign, donate, or keep. I suggest doing that exercise four times a year during each season until you have pared down your wardrobe to what fits well and is essential.

Before deciding what to keep, consider the popular concept of a capsule wardrobe, which is a small collection of high quality pieces that do not go out of fashion. Outfits are interchangeable and can be dressed up or down depending on the occasion. Women might enjoy Courtney Carver's Project 333™, the minimalist fashion challenge that invites you to dress with thirty-three items or less for three months. Guys can check out Peter Nguyen's website, The Essential Man, a minimalist wardrobe for men.

In the *Inc.* article "Why Successful People Wear the Same Thing Every Day," author Craig Bloem notes that "the average person makes 35,000 decisions every day … A simple way to save brain power is to cut down on the number of decisions you need to make." Bloem mentioned Barack Obama, Mark Zuckerberg, and Steve Jobs as examples of men who wear similar clothing each day. Greg McKeown echoes Bloem in his book *Essentialism*: "The preponderance of choice has overwhelmed our ability to manage it. We have lost our ability to filter what is important and what isn't. Psychologists call this 'decision fatigue': the more choices we are forced to make, the more the quality of our decisions deteriorates."

Perhaps it is easier for men to have fewer clothes, like Steve Jobs wearing jeans and a black turtleneck and Mark Zuckerberg wearing his grey T-shirt or hoodie. Women may feel differently and want splashes of color and accessories and jewelry. But I suspect whatever your gender, you might have clothes that no longer flatter you or that you do not like anymore. Your closets may be jammed full and drawers may be crammed with old, tired clothing. Experiment with reducing the number of your clothing options. Perhaps you will gain more focus on other parts of your life that are more important to you. Furthermore, by practicing decluttering little things, you may gain confidence in your capabilities for making bigger decisions.

Kitchen and Food Waste

If I had to guess, based on cleaning out my parents' homes, most kitchen contents could be cut in half. As I have downsized myself a few times, I am amazed how many duplicates I find in my kitchen. I had a plethora of knives and plastic storage containers. I had a collection of knives designed for every conceivable single task or food group. In reality, I used only three of them regularly. I was able to pare down to about three containers for leftovers as well. I got rid of cookbooks I hadn't opened in a year.

I also found items I had saved from my parents' kitchen clean outs that I thought were potentially useful. I saved gadgets that help arthritic hands, for example. Because I have become increasingly scrupulous about the contents of my home, I decided that I would rather give those handy but unused things to someone who could use them right now. If I need them later, I can seek them out then. I focus on having fewer, high quality utensils and kitchen tools.

I am also not a fan of bulk buying. Once the kids were grown, I gradually phased out purchasing large quantities of supplies. I keep a few snacks and cans of soup or other nonperishable items to get me through a snowstorm or a few days of staying home. But otherwise, I shop more frequently and plan a week at a time for my cooking needs. Furthermore, my new place does not have a pantry, so there really isn't room to stockpile food.

I have a pet peeve about food waste. I am vigilant about what I put into my refrigerator, and it is rare that I find anything spoiled. When we toss food, we squander our money and our nonrenewable resources, such as water and fossil fuels. Greenhouse gas emissions are emitted from our landfills as food is incinerated or decomposes. The article "10 Shocking Food Waste Statistics" revealed the problem in America:

- Americans throw away $165 billion worth of food each year.
- Forty percent of food is wasted in the United States every year.
- Thirty-five million tons of food are wasted in the United States each year.
- The average American household throws away $2,200 worth of food each year.
- The average American throws away 300 pounds of food per year.
- More than twenty pounds of food is wasted per person every month in the United States.
- Twenty percent of food that the average American buys is never eaten.
- Ninety percent of food is thrown away too soon.
- Food waste in American has grown by 204 percent since 1960 and fifty percent since 1990.
- Reducing food waste by just fifteen percent would be enough to feed more than twenty-five million Americans every year.

Thankfully, there are some enterprising people and organizations that reroute food to the hungry, and you can research those by searching the internet for "repurpose food waste" to learn more about programs near you. But, as a starting point, assess your own kitchen and food-buying habits and trim waste from within your home. If you thin out multiple kitchen gadgets, for example, you can give them to groups that collect and give kitchen supplies to refugees who may have come to your country with nothing and are starting over to build a life. This is one way to simultaneously declutter your home and give to those in need.

Despite still having a junk drawer, I love having a tidy kitchen. I found it particularly insightful when I removed absolutely everything from each cabinet and shelf in my kitchen and refrigerator. I then cleaned the area and only put back the essential items and the ones I actually used. When I put my big house on the market, in order to downsize, my realtor staged my home for showings. Invariably, my agent wanted clean and uncluttered countertops. It looks better to potential buyers, and I realized it feels better for me to keep it that way too. Since we use our kitchen several times a day, it is a good room to clean and declutter.

Gifts

I am a fan of the book *The Five Love Languages* by Gary Chapman. I respect that gifts are one of those five languages and people with that language feel love when giving or receiving gifts. At this point, given my minimizing mindset and lifestyle, I prefer to give and receive consumable gifts, such as food or to share a meal or an experience.

Swedish author Margareta Magnusson writes, "I do know people who maintain what we in Sweden call a fulskåp, a cabinet for the ugly. A fulskåp is a cupboard full of gifts you can't stand to look at, and which are impossible to regift. Usually these are presents from distant aunts and uncles that you put on display when the giver comes to visit. This is a bad idea." I agree it is not wise to keep these items, but it can be difficult to let go of feeling guilty for getting rid of unwanted gifts.

Marie Kondo also talks about gifts. "Presents are not 'things' but a means for conveying someone's feelings. When viewed from this perspective, you don't need to feel guilty for parting with a gift. Just thank it for the joy it gave you when you first received it."

I am now at a point where I discuss holidays and birthdays in advance with family and friends. If there is something I really want or need, I let a potential gift giver know. Otherwise, I suggest something we can do together, such as dining out. If the person is not in close proximity and feels the need to give, I suggest something like a gift card to my favorite restaurant or coffee shop. Rethinking how you exchange gifts may also help you maintain only the essential items in your home.

I have extracted myself from the craziness of Christmas shopping. I boycott commercialism during the holidays. I ignore Black Friday, and I do not go to shopping malls, although I support individual artisans. I focus on minimizing stress and overspending during that time of year. For me, I love to go to parties and hang out with friends and relatives. I reflect on the past year and celebrate with those people who have been a part of my life. Shopping for gifts feels burdensome, and as a result, I have weaned myself away from the practice. Sharing experiences rather than exchanging gifts feels much more rewarding.

Catalogs, Magazines, and Books

When I decided to minimize my stuff, I also became a gatekeeper of what came into my mailbox. I unsubscribed to every magazine except one, *Tennis*. I enjoy keeping up with the players I watch on TV and see in person when I attend a professional tournament. I also called every catalog company from which I received a mailing. I asked that my name and address be removed from their database. I simultaneously contacted banks and asked to receive statements electronically. As far as the other junk mail I received, I got myself taken off all paper mailings for solicitations. I eliminated all store credit cards and their sales promotions. This was a somewhat time-consuming process, but ultimately almost all of the junk mail stopped. I no longer have to view or discard massive amounts of paper and mail I don't care about. I only receive vital information and greeting cards from friends.

An advantage of not getting catalogs is the removal of any buying temptation. I had already quit shopping for anything other than food and absolute necessities. Advertisements in magazines might have lured me into a purchase of something I did not need. Catalogs or sale postcards can be teasers. It was liberating to receive less junk mail and save a few trees too.

The website Waste Away provides staggering statistics on the environmental effects of junk mail. Here is one of the most shocking ones: "Experts estimate 100 million trees are used every year just to produce junk mail … The forests on the earth absorb two billion tons of carbon a year. But with the deforestation needed for junk mail, there are fewer trees to help reduce greenhouse gases."

The website suggests that you can help to stop this environmental tragedy by contacting one or all of the organizations below:

- 41pounds.org
- Paperkarma (an app available for iPhones and Androids)
- Directmail.com
- Catalogchoice.org
- Dmachoice.org
- Optoutprescreen.com

I am not sure about the accuracy of that number of trees being destroyed, but it does make sense to reduce mailings that are useless to me.

Books are a bit more challenging for me to thin out. I am a voracious reader, and I have purchased many books over the course of my life. I have even kept one college textbook on human anatomy. I love holding paperbacks in my hands and often highlight passages. However, I am utilizing the library and reading electronically more often now. I regularly whittle down the number of books I own to a few treasured ones. Seeing a small bookshelf of my favorite books brings me pleasure. My local library and used bookstore happily accept my donations when I thin out my collection. Plus, by checking out books and shopping at used bookstores, I am supporting local institutions I find to be valuable.

Marie Kondo shares a good way to view books: "Books you have read have already been experienced, and their content is inside you." Furthermore, she offers this advice with regard to discarding unread books: "You may have wanted to read it when you bought it, but if you haven't read it by now, the book's purpose was to teach you that you didn't need it. There's no need to finish reading books that you only got halfway through. Their purpose was to be read halfway. So get rid of all those unread books. It will be far better for you to read the book that really grabs you right now than one that you left to gather dust for years."

It still challenges me to thin out my book collection because I worry I might want a discarded book in the future. And one time I did want to reference a book I had given away, but I solved the problem by checking the book out at the library.

Music

My taste in music continues to change as I age. In the past, a particular musician or band might have been magical to me. But today, they've lost favor, and they don't move me anymore. In 2017, I rounded up my CDs and cassette tapes and spread all 187 of them out on the floor. Because my habits had shifted to listening to the radio and using music apps on my phone, most of my collection of tapes had been untouched for years. While I sorted, I picked a few favorites and played them throughout the day. If I found I loved the whole CD, such as the greatest hits from Sheryl Crow or U2, I kept them. If only one or two songs were of interest, I added those songs to my electronic library and placed that CD into the donation pile. I followed the same procedure with my collection of vinyl albums. Yes, I still have a turntable! And I confess that I have a collection from my youth that I decided to keep: twenty-three Barbra Streisand records.

Papers

When I first read Marie Kondo's suggestion to discard all paper, I laughed out loud. She said, "My basic principle for sorting papers is to throw them all away … After all, they will never inspire joy, no matter how carefully you keep them." In my big house, I had a large office with an enormous desk with drawers filled with files. On one wall was built-in cabinetry and bookshelves reaching the ceiling. All of it was full of papers, books, and stuff.

When I downsized in 2012, my new home contained no office at all. I didn't think it was possible to go from a huge office space to none, but I did. On the paper front, I reduced from multiple file drawers to one collapsible one containing only the present year's paperwork that would be necessary for tax preparation or accounting. By switching most bills to electronic versions, I was able to adapt to a small portable file folder that fit into my computer bag with my laptop. I also scanned and digitized documents of importance. I repurposed a small wooden side table with three drawers into the storage space for office supplies. I placed my laptop onto the dining table, and I was done.

When I cleaned out my dad's tall file cabinet at the time of his death, I realized that 90 percent of those papers went into the trash bin. My dad loved to clip articles from newspapers and magazines and then file those in folders with each specific topic on the label. Because his points of interest were not mine, they became obsolete upon his death. Before I discarded the contents of the file cabinet, I brought many boxes full of papers to my home and systematically went through each one. It was a tedious experience. I realized that if I kept a file cabinet with my unique interests, one day, my daughters would have to spend their time doing the same unpleasant task.

My solution was to take my interests and write books about them. I took mountains of research and experience and consolidated them into a readable form that not only my daughters could enjoy but the public as well. Sadly, much of my dad's intellectual knowledge went into a re-cycle bin and not into a form that could live beyond his death. Now, I realize not everyone aspires to write a book. But if you have a passion for a topic, consider gifting that knowledge into a book and toss the papers.

Garage

In my big house phase, I had a three-car garage. When I first moved into that big house in 1996, I was married and had two little kids. My husband and I each had a car, and we used the other stall for bicycles, lawn care equipment, trash cans, and recycle bins. We also had shelving and cabinets filled with tools and toys.

I decided to downsize in 2012 because I was entering the empty nest phase of life. The home I chose to move into had no garage. The thought of going from a three-car garage to none at all was a bit daunting at first; it might be considered impossible by many. But I did it! Everything except essentials had to go away, and I had to find new places to store what I kept.

My new house had a porch. My snow and garden shovel, leaf rake, and broom were either on top of it or under it, depending on the season. My smaller gardening tools went onto a shelf in my laundry closet. I hired someone to mow the lawn. I borrowed from neighbors if there was something I needed but didn't own. Sharing items with neighbors can create community and goodwill. Why did I previously think I had to personally own everything?

When I was in the midst of marriage and raising kids, I would have told you a garage was a necessity. And perhaps it was for the lifestyle I had developed. When I was in the middle of it, I didn't feel the weight of the garage contents. Only after years of not owning and caring for the contents was I able to sense the lightness of not having all that stuff. I only kept what was absolutely necessary, and 99 percent of the rest wasn't needed at all. Occasionally, when I have to dig my car out of snow, I miss the shelter aspect of a garage. And I had to get a good battery for starting the car in cold temperatures. But I grew to appreciate a little exercise and connection to snow that clearing my car provided me a few months a year. I can rent or borrow a bike, and I can purchase one if testing a loaner bike sparks a renewed desire to ride more often. But I still don't need or miss a garage. And I never thought I would say that!

CHAPTER THREE

Enrich or Ditch?

When I first started decluttering, I intentionally did not deal with the sentimental parts of my life, those things that carried an emotional charge. Eventually, after making substantial progress on mundane items, I finally felt ready to tackle the tougher stuff. In addition to asking myself if something was a benefit or a burden for me to keep or if it was superfluous, I also questioned if it enriched my life *now*. If the answer was no, I ditched it.

Marie Kondo says, "But when we really delve into the reasons for why we can't let something go, there are only two: an attachment to the past or a fear for the future." So I examined my past and looked at my future to clear areas I had resisted before. I even found humor, laughing at myself on occasion.

Abandoned Hobbies, Sports Equipment, Pet Ashes, and the Potentially Useful

Former sports or hobbies may have been a big part of your life, but for whatever reason, you moved on to other endeavors. Due to fond memories or the thought of perhaps doing it again, you may have kept stuff you haven't touched in years. When I read: "If you have it, use it. If you don't use it, don't have it" from the book *The Art of Discarding* by Nagisa Tatsumi, I took the advice to heart. Here are a few examples:

Crafts

I once took classes in knitting, crocheting, and quilting when I was in my twenties. I created scarves, blankets, and quilted bedspreads. Then I stopped doing those crafts. I was too busy with motherhood. Years went by, and I never picked up those hobbies again. I eventually donated a box of knitting and crochet needles and extra yarn and fabric to someone who could use them.

Artistic Endeavors

In my twenties, I traveled to Santa Fe, New Mexico, with my husband. We visited many art studios, and I became enamored with sculptures. I decided (with no past artistic background) that I would become a sculptor. I bought two bags of clay to begin my new passion. After several years of storing these heavy bags of unsculpted clay and moving them to a new house, I realized that my whim of artistic fancy was unlikely to come to reality. I finally donated the clay to an art shop.

Ice Skates

I took my pretty white ice skates from my youth along with me everywhere I lived until age fifty-four. I actually tried skating with them a few times when I was fifty, but they hurt my feet (they were a little small), and my trip to the ice rink did not rekindle my love of ice-skating enough to return. Nonetheless, I kept the skates a few more years until I finally said goodbye to them. If I ever go skating again, I can rent skates that fit the size of my feet now.

Golf Clubs

I took golf lessons in college and thought I liked the sport. I bought some fairly inexpensive clubs. A few years of haphazard playing with little improvement followed. I then decided that I liked other sports much better and would consider taking up the sport again when I got older. Golf is still not calling me, so I recently donated the clubs to an auction for a good cause.

Pet Ashes

I kept my beloved dog's ashes in a metal tin. It felt too hard to do anything with them. After eleven years, I found the ability to place them outside in a burial plot for a cat I had laid to rest. I planted flowers around this area that added a colorful swath of blooms for passersby and myself to enjoy. But I kept one memento: her collar.

Towrope

My dad gave me a towrope decades ago. I transferred it to every car I had since I received it. Finally, I admitted that I had not taken it out of the plastic packaging and didn't plan to tow anyone. I have an auto protection plan with towing services, and so I am unlikely to use this potentially useful gift. I gave it to a friend with a truck.

Boxes and Plastic Bags

My mom used to save all the boxes that her electrical or technical appliances came in. She thought those boxes might be useful if she moved. They took up a lot of space in her basement, and I finally convinced her that they needed to go, and she agreed to let me recycle them. She also seemed to have kept every plastic bag that entered her home. She reused many of them for trash bags, but when I cleared her house, I found dozens of bags in every part of her home. I donated or discarded those bags and have moved to a practice of bringing reusable bags to the grocery store when I shop.

Instruction Manuals for Appliances

After I install a microwave or television and am using it without confusion, I discard instruction manuals. I used to keep stacks of them for every appliance in the house. But

I never referred to them again once they were placed in a drawer. If I should ever possibly need a manual again, I can look it up online for the make and model in question.

I have yet to regret discarding any of these items. If I get the urge to do those hobbies or sports again, I can have fun taking a class to refresh my memory. If my enthusiasm returns, I can add the necessary equipment or tools then. I am becoming better at releasing the "what-ifs" that clog my closets.

Sentimental and Historical Stuff

This part of our stuff can be most challenging to deal with, and it might be best saved for last in your clearing process. I had many boxes of sentimental and historical items to sort. Here is how I tackled some tough spots:

Souvenirs
I used to collect souvenirs from theater performances, concerts, festivals, and travel. My focus is now on the experience and less on gathering things such as T-shirts, trinkets, and programs. I admit that I still occasionally buy a coffee cup on a trip, and I have framed some posters of the Breckenridge Film Festival. But I try to be mindful about which mementos I keep.

Love Letters
In a fit of anger and hurt, most of the love notes and cards from my ex-husband were discarded at the time of

my divorce. One loving note survived to the present, and I decided to keep it so that my daughters could read a note from their dad to me that expressed love.

In the many years since my divorce, I have had a few meaningful relationships. I kept love letters from two men in a shoebox. I occasionally opened the box and read a few pages. Recently, I decided to let them go. Before I discarded them, I held them to my heart and thanked those guys for the love they expressed to me. Even though I did not keep their notes, I kept their thoughts in my heart with appreciation.

Greeting Cards

I had developed the habit of discarding the previous year's Christmas cards as I prepared to send new ones each December. Gradually through the years, I had gotten rid of most other cards, such as birthday cards. But I had a hard time disposing of cards from my parents. But how many did I need to keep? In my less-is-more philosophy, I decided to keep four or five cards or notes from my parents. I was particularly drawn to the ones that said "I love you" since that sentiment was infrequently verbalized when I was growing up, despite having a nice childhood.

Graduation, Wedding, Baby, and Funeral Announcements

I had the habit of keeping every announcement that I received when I reached adulthood. At age fifty-five, I opened that box and looked at each one. I paused to remember the person or reflect on a birth, or death, or landmark event. I laughed when I found one announcement of someone I couldn't remember. Was I losing my mind or did that person drop out of my life long ago into oblivion? Also in that box, I found extra copies of my own wedding and birth announcements. I framed my daughter's birth announcements, and put the wedding program into a scrapbook, and recycled the rest. I now only keep those announcements until I attend the event or send a card or gift.

Scrapbooks and Yearbooks

I am not a big scrapbook person, but I have a few. One was from my summer camp days as a kid. I really enjoyed looking at it and decided to keep it for now. My daughters also went to that camp, so they might get a kick out of looking at it too. I compiled another scrapbook for a business venture, but I didn't reach my success goals. As my priorities shifted to a writing career, I lost interest in that business. I spent time looking through the scrapbook and appreciating that period of my life and the friendships and growth that occurred. I then tossed the book.

As far as my yearbooks, I still have them. I love high school reunions, and I always attend them every ten years. I review the yearbooks before and after those events with much enjoyment, so I decided to keep them. A few years ago, I brought my middle school yearbooks to a gathering of my childhood friends. My intention was to throw them out after that get-together. We passed them around, reminisced, and laughed a lot. I was so surprised by how much we enjoyed looking at those awkward years that I did not throw them out after all! But for those who do not attend reunions or have not kept in touch with childhood friends, it may be easy for you to discard your yearbooks.

Awards, Diplomas, Metals, and Trophies

Most achievement relics have been thrown out. I scanned or placed some paper certificates that held more significance to me into a photo album about my life to give to my daughters. My university diploma is framed and in our family's Hall of Fame, along with my daughter's diplomas.

I took pictures of my swimming medals and trophies from my youth. I held a cheap plastic trophy from my teenage years in the 1970s when I was on a summer swim team. It said "Most Valuable," which meant a lot to me. I reconnected to the wonderful feeling I experienced when I was given that trophy at age seventeen. Letting that one go was a little difficult, but the feeling and memories remain with me. I can always look at the photo of it if I want to remind myself of that achievement.

In my adulthood, I played in many tennis tournaments. I amassed a lot of trophies. But over time, I placed them into boxes instead of displaying them. I again took a picture of them and let them go. The only ones I kept were practical ones that were drinking glasses or mugs that I could use in the kitchen. When the fires of my competitive drive had diminished, these mementos held less meaning for me, which made it easier to relinquish them.

My daughters grew up in an era when trophies were given out to every kid who participated on a sports team. These trophies were particularly meaningless, and my girls threw those out too. I cringe to think about how many cheap, plastic trophies sit in landfills!

My Children's Things

If you have reached midlife and have an empty nest like me, you will be confronted with many things related to raising children. In retrospect, it would have been easier if I had not stored baby gear but rather released items after each phase had passed. Marie Kondo provided this perspective: "When you come across something that you cannot part with, think carefully about its true purpose in your life. You'll be surprised at how many of the things you possess have already fulfilled their role. By acknowledging their contribution and letting them go with gratitude, you will be able to truly put the things you own, and your life, in order. In the end, all that will remain are the things that you really treasure. To truly cherish the things that are important to you, you must first discard those that have outlived their purpose."

At times while raising children, I placed some of their things, such as cute baby clothes or toys, into boxes. I also kept some of my daughters' artwork. While deciding which of these things I would let go of, my touch-everything philosophy required I open every box and spread the contents out on my dining table. Despite being time-consuming, I picked up each and every item in those boxes. I assessed my feelings and whether or not the purpose of that thing had passed. And I paused to allow memories to surface. Regarding artwork, less is more. Keeping a few favorite pieces was enough. I didn't need to keep every school project and drawing.

(Confession regarding my own childhood toys: I kept one item—a stuffed Snoopy.)

Diaries

For ten straight years, I wrote in a diary from age fourteen to twenty-four. I have wanted to toss them out several times but haven't done it yet. I occasionally pick one up and read a few pages. Who was that inarticulate girl who used four adjectives to describe everything: dull, dumb, sick, and weird? I wish I could say the entries were filled with profound wisdom like Anne Frank's diaries, but I had yet to record my thoughts and feelings with much depth. For now, I keep them, since I have not yet carved out the time to really assess the contents. Furthermore, my oldest daughter has expressed interest in them. So, they remain in a box for future analysis.

Family History

I am interested in genealogy. Being entrusted with recording and maintaining our family history, I keep a few

records and photo albums to pass down to future generations. I took the time to organize the stuff that came into
my hands. I have one plastic bin that contains the whittled
down materials that I deemed of most interest. Again, I
scanned many photos and shared digital albums with
other family members. I suspect that future generations
will want only the condensed version and are unlikely to
spend time organizing a mess. So, if I want the history to
live on, I better get it straightened out to the best of my
abilities now!

Photos

My dad loved photos and passed that passion down
to me. However, he didn't organize them. He had many
duplicate photos, and he stashed them in different places
throughout his house. I gathered, scanned, and placed
them into albums. I hired a professional company to con-
vert the slides to digital as well. I did this organizing to
honor my dad and to be able to pass down his storied
life to our family. I also created a pictorial collection of my
mom's life while I was in the mode of sorting.

The experience of creating albums for my parents
spurred my awareness that it would be a gift to my daughters if I took the initiative of organizing my own photos. I
threw out poor quality pictures. I kept a few shots of me
with crazy hair or in some comedic situation, but otherwise, if I looked horrible, I threw the picture away.

I continue to curate the photo albums I created because even those have redundancy. Furthermore, there

are pictures of people whose names I cannot remember. If the era that I photographed doesn't have any special significance to me anymore, or if my daughters will find the photos meaningless, I also remove them. Even though I will continue to assess and reduce the number of my pictures regularly, they are in a state of organization now, which gives me peace of mind.

Wedding Dress

I loved my wedding dress and all that it represented. I was twenty-five when I got married, and I was thrilled. After the wedding, my mom took the dress and had it professionally cleaned and boxed to save. I thought my daughters might want it one day. The box traveled from house to house wherever I moved after 1988.

Finally, as I approached what would have been my thirtieth wedding anniversary, I was ready to let it go. I took it out of the box and put it on. It still fit my body, but it didn't fit my life. My daughters didn't want it, and I couldn't blame them. If they decided to get married, they would want to create a wedding of their choosing and a look that was fresh and unique to them. In January of 2019, I donated the dress to a consignment bridal store. Because I had done my grieving and processing by then, donating the dress was just a giant relief.

I chuckled when I realized the irony that men just rent a tuxedo for their weddings, while women usually spend a lot of money and then have to figure out what to do with their dress for years thereafter. It would have been so much easier if I had released the dress shortly after getting married. Realistically, I would never wear it again. I just went along with tradition without really thinking about what it would require of me in terms of maintenance and emotional turmoil.

Heirlooms and Collections

The Great Depression had an enormous influence on both of my parents. They were frugal and saved things just in case they could be used again someday. Both my parents had collections of things in large quantities that were of interest to them. Over the decades, after their divorce in 1977, they gradually filled up their homes.

My dad's second career was as a rancher, and he acquired many things relating to horses, cattle, and ranch life. My dad was also a history buff and had many items relating to his service in World War II. As such, his living room held an impressive display of items that held no personal interest for me. The war occurred before I was born, and the ranching phase of his life happened after my parents' divorce, when I was older and pursuing interests of my own.

On the other hand, my mom had collections of the finer things in life, such as silver tea sets and silverware, as well as crystal table settings. These beautiful items filled a china hutch and cabinets. They were pretty to look at but, like my father's memorabilia, were also not of interest to me. I preferred a more practical and modern dining set and far fewer items. I was told that my grandmother entertained with tea services regularly. This lifestyle had not been passed down through the generations to me, and so these items were not ones I wanted to inherit.

My dad passed away in 2015, just shy of his ninetieth birthday. I found myself as the family member in charge of emptying the house. As I was grieving his loss, I was simultaneously immersed in the arduous task of finding a new home for a mass quantity of things. Some of it was museum quality, some of it was junk, and the rest of it was everything in between. I was overwhelmed with the responsibility of dispersing his belongings.

My sister helped take junk to the trash bins. As I mentioned earlier, one of my brothers took my dad's Western collection. I gave some things to friends and donated to charities. I also provided items to a museum for the ranch that my dad had sold to his county's open space. I succeeded in clearing his home but with a heavy emotional toll. I did my best to honor my dad and find good new homes for his possessions, but I continue to process and heal from his death and its aftermath.

In 2018, my mom was no longer able to live in her home. She moved to an assisted living facility. I once again found myself in a position of clearing a parental home when I had barely recovered from my dad's death. My family took a few things, but we already had full houses and didn't need much. And nobody wanted the fine crystal and silver collections.

Because my dad passed away before his home was emptied, he did not have to witness the lack of interest and dissipation of some of his cherished possessions. I suspect it would have been painful for him. But my mom was still alive and mentally sound, so she watched and felt the anguish of her things disappearing. She had a heavy heart, trying to understand why the younger generation didn't want these family things.

I attempted to find good homes for her things, especially my grandparents' heirlooms. Both my parents and my grandparents were from the small town of Wessington Springs, South Dakota. This rural town contained a Shakespeare gardens and a replica of Anne Hathaway's cottage. The cottage is now a museum and occasionally hosts events, including tea services. The women in charge of the cottage willingly accepted the silver and crystal tea sets my mom had preserved. They sent my mom a thank you note that warmed her heart and provided some relief during a difficult process. And I suspect my grandmother would have smiled approval that her precious treasures were being used once again for tea services.

Each family member took a thing or two that was useful or meaningful. My mom gladdened when something found its way into our lives. But she came to the painful realization that most of her home contents were not wanted. The article "Sorry, Parents: Nobody Wants the Family 'Heirlooms'" appeared on the website Apartment Therapy on August 21, 2017. Author Melissa Massello captured the attitudes of younger generations with regard to inheriting items from older generations: "We want to start and curate *our own* collections—we want to be surrounded by pieces that are curated to reflect *our* travels, *our* memories, *our* ways of entertaining, and *our* personal styles." That sentiment nailed my feelings and those of my millennial daughters.

Massello went on to say, "But, like many younger to middle age Americans, we don't want to have to pay movers by the box or rent storage units by the month just to be able to pass on the things hoarded and left behind by others. We'd rather tell their stories or show a picture of them without having to actually live with, and deal with, and pay for keeping All. That. Stuff … Please, don't guilt your kids into keeping all (or any) of your stuff."

It is a harsh reality to fantasize that others will share interest in your own collections. In some cases, it happens, such as one of my brothers taking many of Dad's cowboy and Indian valuables. My other brother and I kept some World War II items. I kept one box containing sterling silver utensils and one dozen medium-sized crystal plates from my mom. My hope is that because I attempted to find good places and charities for the rest of my parents' heirlooms and collections that someone, who does love that sort of thing, will use and enjoy them. Perhaps special pieces will take on new life in a new family. That thought eased my mom's mind and my conscience.

The flip side of hanging onto parents' heirlooms is that there might be fighting among family members about who gets what. Because of greed or guilt, or because someone wants to control the process, there are often estrangements. The glue that once held a family together can weaken without a plan and clear wishes that are expressed and documented.

There is nothing wrong with creating a collection. The search and addition of a new piece can be enjoyable to the collector. But it behooves the person gathering things to realize that their family might not share that particular passion and that those items might ultimately be owned by someone outside of the descendants. As I thin out my things and discuss what to do with what is left, I release the expectation that they must be passed down within my family. This openness and acceptance may potentially pave the way for less disputes and resentments in the future.

Having just a few of each of my parents' things ensures that I see, use, and appreciate them. By having less, what I keep is special. I think of each parent or grandparent when my eyes rest upon that thing that somehow made it through the cleanout process of past homes. That heirloom may sit on the fireplace mantle, hang on the wall, or be put to use. I strive to honor past generations while acknowledging the unique personalities and lifestyles of current and future generations. And, as this book advocates, I am careful not to overload my daughters with the monumental task of dealing with too much of my stuff that was never sorted during my lifetime.

Be mindful and prevent possible conflict surrounding your belongings. Aging often produces a waning of energy, and sadly, not all of us will maintain a sound mind. Possible disability, mental or physical, can relegate sorting and dispersing one's belongings to someone else who might not want the job. A comprehensive book that goes into detail on how to liquidate an estate or anticipate what that process involves is *The Boomer Burden* by Julie Hall. Read it before you need it. Hall sums it up nicely: "Don't set your kids up for a big fight and a dumpster load of ill feelings! Begin right now taking steps to give your kids the best final gift any parent can give: a peaceful final farewell and a loving legacy."

CHAPTER FOUR

Additional Considerations

Clutter is usually associated with the objects we stuff into our homes. However, clutter and disorganization can find their way into many other dimensions of our lives. As I tidied my house, other messes became obvious. Once I was in the mode of decluttering, I added additional areas of my life to sort and organize. This portion of the book addresses other aspects of our lives that might merit cleaning up and simplifying.

Financial

One's money situation can be complicated or in disarray. Couples often have differing views on handling money. When I was married, my husband was in a constant state of leveraging our money for real estate acquisitions.

I preferred to be debt free. It was stressful to navigate such differing views.

Since I am the one writing this book, my bias is skewed toward debt-free living. But I acknowledge there are reasons one might have debt, especially a home mortgage or student loan. Spending on everyday purchases is more of my focus. Dave Ramsey wrote *The Total Money Makeover*. He said, "It is human nature to want it and want it now ... Being willing to delay pleasure for a greater result is a sign of maturity." I suspect much of the debt in our society is a result of wanting instant gratification. Our homes might be full of things we bought on an impulse.

If you desire to simplify your financial spending and reduce your temptations on gathering more stuff, consider cutting up all of your credit cards, except one or two. I have two cards: one for personal purchases and one for business expenses. And I pay those cards off each month. Better yet, try a year of cash-only spending and cease shopping at malls or online. Living a cash lifestyle can facilitate new, healthy money management habits. Differentiation between essential purchases and frivolous ones may become more apparent if one pays in full without a credit card.

Financial planners can provide assistance in crunching the numbers for a long-range forecast of the money you will need in your senior years. Budgets can help you reach your objectives now and for your retirement. A plan aligned with your values and goals can help you track your progress and make adjustments as needed for changes in life circumstances. Once you have sorted through your finances and created priorities, your choices for expenditures will have more clarity as you focus on your vision for your future.

Legal and Estate Documents

A will and estate plan can be done at any age. One can create a paper and a digital copy of important paperwork. Key family members can be granted access digitally or told where to find paper documents. If trust is an issue, an attorney can keep your documents. Family members can then be directed to contact that person in the event of your disability or death.

Here is a list to consider completing as you tidy up your affairs:

- Last will and testament
- Powers of attorney—general and medical
- Digital assets access authorization form
- Advance directive—planning for important health care decisions
- HIPAA privacy authorization form
- Information and instructions of business dealings and financial institutions
- Key contact list of professionals/doctors
- Key contact list of friends and organizations

- Other personal wishes and private communications
- Information needed for a death certificate
- Obituary draft
- Declaration of disposition of last remains

If you have already completed all or most of that list, congratulations! If not, I encourage you to organize your estate documents simultaneously with the stuff in your home. Attending to these personal and financial matters can simplify your life and make decisions easier for your loved ones.

Social Media, Email, and Technology

Clutter also exists in our communications. Advances in technology can be simultaneously helpful and overwhelming. There is a lot of noise out there. I have been guilty of posting trivial chatter on social media. But with my focus on clutter reduction, I am becoming more conscious of how often I post and what I say.

Using Facebook and other social media platforms has pros and cons. The benefits for me include feeling connected to my friends and relatives, many of whom live far away. I like to post travel pictures and enjoy looking at the adventures of others. I also learn things, laugh, and feel a part of a community when I browse the News Feed. If I don't check in, I sometimes feel a loss, not knowing what is going on in the world. But I am mindful of the balancing act between virtual and real, in-person interactions.

I log on to my computer in the morning and review email and Facebook. I don't feel I can move on to other things of greater importance like writing until I have cleaned out new emails and briefly reviewed my News Feed on Facebook. However, I cut off browsing and responding by nine a.m. Other people may structure their day the other way, with email and social media as a treat after a productive block of time. Regardless how you use it, remember to set limits on your use of social media, as a way to declutter your life.

I regularly thin out my email, unsubscribing to newsletters and other unwanted notices. I aim for fewer than fifty items in my inbox—and on an efficient day, fewer than twenty. I have created files of important emails to keep as reference, and quarterly I review and weed out obsolete items. I also periodically look at my phone and remove all apps that I have not used in the past six months, and I organize the ones I keep. Perhaps I am an organizational addict, and I am fooling myself into thinking that those measures make me less hooked! But my disciplined organization helps keep my sanity with the constant influx of messages.

It is challenging to keep up with fast-changing technology, new apps, social media, and cell phone options. Is all this fast-paced change helping us? The answer is probably mixed. I love my phone and its capabilities, and I also fondly recall the days before cell phones and computers where I spent more time outside with friends or reading books. I still do all those things, but not as much or as often, and I can be distracted while doing them.

The internet can make us shallow thinkers as we scan for quick information. Our attention scatters as we skim or look for bullet points and hyperlinks. We catch glimpses of advertisements, and in general, rove the page in spurts and jumps. Reading an article without bolding and lists may seem difficult. Reliance on technology can reduce our memory, as we rely on our computers or phones instead of our minds. Can you remember important phone numbers, or do you rely on speed dial and your favorites in your contact list? When was the last time you sat down and read an article from beginning to end and then really thought about it?

In the book *The Shallows: What the Internet Is Doing to Our Brains*, author Nicholas Carr described having more difficulty keeping his attention focused on concentrated reading and deep contemplation. I have been noticing this trend in myself, and it bothers me. My mind drifts, and I am constantly pulling it back into focus. Carr confirms, "When the ditchdigger trades his shovel for a backhoe, his arm muscles weaken, even as his efficiency increases. A similar tradeoff may well take place as we automate the work of the mind."

How can we combat these negatives? I would suggest that awareness is the first step. Ask yourself if your phone or computer is a leash. Do you control them, or do they control you?

In *The Shallows,* Carr also suggests how important it is to periodically step away from our electronic gadgets: "A series of psychological studies over the past twenty years has revealed that after spending time in a quiet, rural setting close to nature, people exhibit greater attentiveness, stronger memory, and generally improved cognition. Their brains become both calmer and sharper. The reason, according to attention restoration theory (ART) is that when people aren't being bombarded by external stimuli, their brains can, in effect, relax. They no longer have to tax the working memories by processing a stream of bottom-up distractions. The resulting state of contemplativeness strengthens their ability to control their mind."

There are a plethora of reasons to unplug from technology, rest our brains, and spend more time in nature. You have my permission to put down this book, leave your cell phone behind, and take a walk outside right now!

Conversation

In conversation, some people are uncomfortable with silence and do anything to fill it. I am practicing allowing space in conversation. If I constantly talk, I may not allow someone to say something they would like to say. I find it wise to discern if the person I am speaking with just needs a good listener or if that person is asking for a fix. I can inquire directly, or I can listen attentively and only offer suggestions if asked directly. Stephen Covey says, "Most people do not listen with the intent to understand; they listen with the intent to reply." I find decluttering leads to quieting my mind and allowing spaces to evolve, all of which helps me be more present.

I focus on quieting my inner mind chatter when someone is talking to me. I feel calm when I don't have to craft a response immediately or solve anything. I do not need to share a similar experience, although sometimes I do. If I can do it briefly without hijacking the conversation, I might interject a thought. But I then redirect back to the person who first began the dialogue. Sometimes I ask more questions to draw out more details or clarify what is being said. The one speaking can often work out their own solution by hearing themselves talk about it with a good listener.

I sometimes get into long stories during conversations. My youngest daughter frequently asks me to get to the point. I understand the merits of not rambling, and I also know that sometimes I work things out by sharing a story. Certain occasions are designed for catching up and telling stories. At other times, I might need to summarize and deliver the message succinctly. Furthermore, I remind myself that some people are extroverts and are energized by talking. Others are introverts and can become depleted with too much talking. Most all of us, including me, can improve our communication and listening skills. As I organize my thoughts and speak with more clarity, I am more efficient with my time, and I can save myself from misunderstandings.

Sustainability and Environmental Impact

Our society has previously pressured home buyers to purchase as big as they can afford—and in some cases bigger, stretching a family's finances and making them more vulnerable to potentially losing it all. That trend was evident when the housing bubble burst in 2008 and foreclosures became rampant. What a disservice to push people beyond their means!

What is the environmental impact of home size? How many square feet does one person or one family need? If you have never had children or your children are grown, what size home would suit you best? How much do you want to clean, heat, cool, and maintain?

I had my big house on the market to sell in the same month my youngest daughter graduated from high school. It sold two months later. In retrospect, I might have benefited financially if I had downsized much sooner. I was not able to clean my big house by myself, so I hired someone to do it for me twice a month. When I moved to a small house, I could eliminate that cost and clean myself. And with less stuff inside my home, it didn't take as much of my time to dust, mop, and vacuum. The cost of heating or cooling drastically lowered in my smaller space. Insurance and property taxes went down as well. Condominium living eliminates yard care such as lawn mowing, raking, snow shoveling, sprinkler system care, and so forth. There may be a homeowner's association fee, but if managed well, it can be reasonable for all the maintenance and services it covers.

Perhaps you have a large family and many grandchildren, and you want to entertain them or wish to have them stay with you when visiting. Some people elect to have an extra bedroom to be able to rent out, host guests, or potentially have a place for a caregiver to sleep.

After I downsized to my mountain home of 1,836 square feet, I realized that I rarely ever went to the basement. I found the actual space I used was 1,224 square feet. So I started to rent out the basement, which provided me with additional income to offset the cost of maintaining the home. It surprised me how good it felt to live in a smaller home.

I have read numerous sustainability articles suggesting that a person may want to consider a living space somewhere between 500–1,000 total square feet. The tiny or small house movement has intrigued me. The structures are generally less than 500 square feet. Some tiny homes are mobile, allowing you to travel. Others are set in communities where amenities are available to share.

People sometimes try to keep up with their neighbors and friends. They see their big new house or new fancy gadgets as measures of success. Not getting the newest version of technology might create a feeling of missing out or falling behind. Being in a constant state of wanting and longing can make one exhausted and never satisfied. However, in my experience, dropping comparisons and becoming thankful for what one has already can be liberating, and may also be more sustainable for the environment.

Perhaps it is time to shift our thinking from overconsumption to conservation and sustainable growth. In his article in *SC Times* titled "The American Dream? Check the Landfill," Paul Bugbee stated, "I suspect in a few thousand years, when archaeologists start digging up our remnants, they'll determine our legacy based upon the garbage that filled our landfills and the colossal amount of consumer waste that occupied our lives. Upon further analysis, they'll discover the demise of our society was directly linked to excess: taking on too much debt to consume more than we needed, which ultimately depleted our available resources and undermined the welfare of future generations."

For most of my life, marketing has influenced me. Today, however, I rarely watch television except for an occasional professional tennis tournament and the Olympics. That decision not only freed up time for me to pursue other interests, but it profoundly reduced my exposure to the latest and greatest gadgets being advertised during commercials. Other people have found ways to manage their time by enjoying a few favorite shows but recording them and skipping the commercials. This is another way to avoid being exposed to items that might increase your debt, as well as your clutter.

I doubt a minimalist mindset will slow the economy. People will continue to spend money, but perhaps they might shift from buying more objects to investing in experiences. Fumio Sasaki says, "Unlike our material possessions, our experiences are inside ourselves, and we can take them with us any place we go. No matter what may happen to us, the experiences are ours to keep."

I am a fan of buying secondhand and used if possible. I also advocate getting to know your neighbors and swapping, sharing, borrowing, and loaning items. Repair if you can before replacing. Sadly, many things today are not built to last. A few years ago, I took my thirty-year-old vacuum cleaner in to be repaired. My duct tape "self-fix" was failing, and I hoped to replace the vacuum hose. The young clerk laughed at me and said no such thing existed. He showed me new models. I took my vacuum away and got another year out of it. I eventually took it to a Goodwill donation drop off after a friend gave me a vacuum, possibility as a pity gift.

I have high-tech friends who love to expose me to devices. I listen with interest and only as a way to keep up with technology. Perhaps when my old-fashioned equipment eventually quits working, I will be better prepared for how to replace it, and I will certainly know who to call for guidance in the future.

The Balance: Consumer Debt Statistics, Causes and Impact reported that "in November 2018, US consumer debt rose 6.7 percent to $3.979 trillion." I am not an economic expert, but my gut tells me that enormous figure cannot be good for our future generations. Is our propensity to keep buying when we are in debt a good financial strategy, personally and globally?

And our waste often ends up in landfills. These landfills can create dangerous greenhouse gases. Toxins often find their way into our soil, rivers, and oceans. How long can our environment stay healthy with unchecked waste? Who will foot the bill for the cleanup of contaminated areas? Of course, recycling helps. But when will our communities and government address this issue with education and increased regulations? And when will individuals shift their thinking and question the merits of consumerism? These are some of the deeper impacts of unchecked, constant buying.

Perhaps there is hope in thinking about the connection of our purchases with the environment. Articles such as "Green Generation: Millennials Say Sustainability Is a Shopping Priority," published by Nielsen, may indicate a trend toward a growing consciousness. I hope the minimalist movement and environmental awareness will open our minds. Let's all consider how our buying habits affect future generations.

Carbon Footprint

According to Wikipedia: "A carbon footprint is historically defined as the total emissions caused by an individual, event, organization, or product, expressed as carbon dioxide equivalent." *Global Stewards, Sustainable Living Tips,* reports that 26 percent of what you buy accounts for the average American's carbon emissions. There are many ways to reduce our footprint, regardless of the size of the home you currently reside in.

Huffington Post published "7 Instant Ways to Reduce Your Carbon Footprint":

1. Stop eating (or eat less) meat
2. Unplug your devices
3. Drive less
4. Don't buy "fast fashion"(the latest fad in clothing)
5. Plant a garden
6. Eat local (and organic)
7. Line dry your clothes

Let's educate ourselves and broaden our understanding of how our habits and buying choices affect the planet. We can make a positive difference every time we open our wallets and with each lifestyle choice we make.

Health

What else is a byproduct of clutter? Joseph Ferrari, a professor of psychology at DePaul University in Chicago, studies the causes of clutter and its impact on emotional well-being. In an article entitled "The Unbearable Heaviness of Clutter," featured in *The New York Times* on January 3, 2019, Ferrari states, "Procrastination is closely tied to clutter because sorting through and tossing items is a task that many people find unpleasant and avoid."

The tendency to delay dealing with an ever-growing amount of stuff that accumulates in our homes is something we can all relate to. Our work and responsibilities seem far more important. But sometimes, there comes a tipping point where we cannot ignore the quantity of things we own, and we sense it is affecting our health. Ferrari goes on to say, "The findings add to a growing body of evidence that clutter can negatively impact mental well-being, particularly among women. Clutter can also induce a physiological response, including increased levels of cortisol, a stress hormone."

If you are not familiar with cortisol, here is a mini-education course from Web MD.

Think of cortisol as nature's built-in alarm system. It's your body's main stress hormone. It works with certain parts of your brain to control your mood, motivation, and fear; but what if you're under con-

stant stress and the alarm button stays on? It can derail your body's most important functions. It can also lead to a number of health problems, including:

- *Anxiety and depression*
- *Headaches*
- *Heart disease*
- *Memory and concentration problems*
- *Problems with digestion*
- *Trouble sleeping*
- *Weight gain*

I have dealt with some of those issues. It makes sense that someone might feel less anxiety and more focus in a tidy environment, and that is my experience. It also seems that the stress of moving and getting rid of things would affect us internally. Louise Hay is the author of many books, including *Heal Your Body A–Z: The Mental Causes for Physical Illness and the Way to Overcome Them*. If you utilize her book, you can look up a problem, and she lists the probable cause, as well as a new thought pattern that may help someone suffering from that ailment.

At times, I have had issues with an irritable bowel. A difficulty in digestion is a complex condition with many causative factors, such as diet and food sensitivities. However, I found it interesting that when I looked up the word "colon" in Hay's book this was the association: "Fear of letting go. Holding on to the past." The word "colitis" represents "the ease of letting go of that which is over."

Perhaps we have underestimated the harm of clutter to our health and well-being.

The Antiaging Movement

In the book *The Woman I Wanted to Be*, Diane Von Furstenberg writes, "My face carries all my memories. Why would I erase them?" The antiaging movement can be a benefit or a burden. Ageism, the discrimination of someone due to age, is real. I understand that those in the workforce are often dealing with that reality and want to look younger to keep their careers. Both men and women engage in measures to maintain a youthful look for their job or for their relationship. Likewise, they may be seeking a new relationship and feel they must look younger to attract a new partner. There are many arguments for the benefits of the antiaging path. I respect those decisions.

But the antiaging direction can also feel like a burden. When I was fifty-five, I decided to stop coloring my hair. I was going to wait until sixty-five, but something snapped in me, and suddenly I was done spending the time and money on it. Plus, I wanted to avoid the toxic chemicals. My hair stylist thought I was crazy when I told her my decision. Ironically, I now receive more compliments on my hair than when I colored it.

I have avoided peer pressure and advertising for Botox, fillers, and other facial treatments. I knew those procedures could be a rabbit hole that, once I went down, would be hard to stop. I accept my age spots and crinkles, but I still apply a small amount of makeup. Being self-employed means I don't need to keep up appearances for a company. I still care about how I look, but much of my day is spent alone writing and researching to bring new books to publication, and so I feel far less pressure to spend time and money on my appearance.

If I added up all the money I had already spent in my life on dying my hair, I would be shocked. If I projected skin treatments on top of that figure, I would be doubly stunned. That allocation of my financial funds, as well as the time required, felt like a burden to me. I decided to send that money to my vacation fund instead.

Philosophically, the term *antiaging* also feels like a struggle to me. I take good care of myself and am dedicated to exercise and healthy habits. But I am not interested in fighting aging because it is a natural part of life. I want to age gracefully, and I accept my mortality. That surrender is not giving up on life. On the contrary, I embrace life because it is precious. I don't want to spend my energy on a battle that I won't win. I choose to savor each stage and age for the benefits it offers me. I try not to pine for the past or fear the future. For me, I focus on who I am and what age I am today. That is within my control. That acceptance calms me and keeps my life simplified.

At a certain point in my future, I may elect to engage in medical minimalism to protect myself from overtreatment. There may come a time when I stop taking every conceivable test and suggested treatment from a medical model that seems fixated on prolonging life. I prefer quality to quantity of years. It is an individual choice, and at some point, I may elect to focus on fewer health interventions.

Internal Clutter

As I decreased the size of my home and the amount of stuff in it, I also began to think more about what I was putting into my body. Fumio Sasaki says, "We often gain weight because we're eating more than our bodies need." Buying more and eating more than we need sometimes are in tandem with each other. Furthermore, eating processed and preserved food with lots of ingredients, many of which we can't pronounce or recognize, may not be sensible. As we consider keeping only quality objects in our homes, we may also want to reduce the junk food entering our bodies. Eating more natural foods, vegetables, fruits, nuts, and pure water can nourish us internally.

A typical Western diet often results in impacted feces. Think of it as a clogged colon. Karen Kingston's book *Clear Your Clutter with Feng Shui* has a chapter about this subject. "A natural progression from clearing clutter in your home is clearing the clutter inside the temple of your own physical body. People who collect clutter on the outside tend to collect it on the inside too, but whereas clutter on the outside can hamper your progress in life, clutter on the inside can have more serious health-threatening or even life-threatening consequences."

It is not in the scope of this book or my expertise to dive deeper into your health. But I wanted to touch upon the correlation that food choices can also be a type of clutter. If the subject matter interests you, I encourage you to research and seek a professional or doctor to learn more.

Feng Shui

Kingston explains Feng Shui as "the art of balancing and harmonizing the flow of natural energies in our surroundings to create beneficial effects in our lives." Kingston uses Feng Shui *bagua grid* "to locate where each aspect of your life is found, in any building you occupy." This grid includes prosperity, career, relationships, health, and much more. When these grids are laid out in your home or a room in your home, you can see where your stacked boxes, jammed closets, and clutter falls within the grid. Removing that congestion may impact the corresponding part of your life by freeing the energy of that sector. She states, "Every aspect of your life is anchored energetically in your living space, so clearing clutter can completely transform your entire existence."

Perhaps you have dismissed the concept of Feng Shui as wacky. However, I found a few aspects that particularly resonated with me. Kingston says, "A cluttered basement symbolizes issues from the past not dealt with." My basement was often where I put things that I was not ready to let go of, such as baby paraphernalia, my wedding dress, kids' artwork, and boxes of my dad's photographs. Because of my downsizing efforts and lack of storage, I finally dealt with those tough-to-release items. A sense of heaviness lifted as I processed that time of my life.

Before I dived into a round of decluttering, I often experienced a vicious cycle that kept me feeling disempowered and tired. Kingston says, "Clutter accumulates when energy stagnates, and likewise, energy stagnates when clutter accumulates. So the clutter begins as a symptom of what is happening with you in your life and then becomes part of the problem itself because the more of it you have, the more stagnant energy it attracts to itself."

Even if you are a skeptic, you can test out the theory by removing a cluster of clutter from an area of your home, and see if anything changes in your life in the coming months. If you are intrigued by the concept of Feng Shui, study the concepts or hire an expert to help you. Your clearing efforts may affect your life in ways you never imagined.

Packing for Evacuation

My mountain home is in an area where forest fires occasionally occur. A few years ago, a fire started nearby and my town was placed on a pre-evacuation status: we were instructed to pack our cars and be ready to leave at a moment's notice. While the winds were blowing the flames toward town, I had to quickly decide what to put in my car. The results of that rushed packing somewhat surprised me.

I love art, and I did place some of my favorite paintings into the car. I also put my dancing boots and swim and tennis gear into the car. Those things were replaceable, but I wanted to continue doing the activities and sports I loved if I were displaced. I also took my laptop to continue writing and communicating.

Thankfully, the winds reversed direction, and the fire went back onto itself instead of coming into town. None-theless, our pre-evacuation status remained in place for three tense days. After the crisis passed, I took further measures to preserve what mattered most to me and get rid of what didn't. Thinning out my mountain home clar-ified what was junk, what was neutral, and what I really cared about. By getting rid of meaningless things around my home, I could see and grab the good stuff easily if time allowed and there was another evacuation situation. And I continue to digitize and remotely save pictures and documents for preservation. If you have never thought about what to grab during an evacuation, it might be a worthy exercise to consider.

Chapter Five

Lifelong Decluttering and Simplifying

Once I was immersed in decluttering, I found that it became a lifestyle choice. I looked toward my future and made decisions to simplify for ease and peace of mind. Lightening my load of stuff and responsibilities freed me to look forward to planning and creating a living situation that was sustainable and lessened potential stress in caring for a home and its contents as I aged.

Progressive Downsizing

As I previously mentioned, in 2012, I downsized from a 5,567-square-foot home with a three-car garage to an 1,836-square-foot house with no garage. In 2019, I bought a second home. You may at first glance think I had regressed in my minimalist direction with that acquisition.

To explain this decision, I will share my vision for the future. Because I have observed two parents go from vital, active people to stages of fragility and disability prior to death, I know that if I live into my elder years, the same thing will happen to me. My 1,836-square-foot mountain home in Breckenridge, Colorado, sits at an elevation of 9,600 feet. The home has a steep staircase to reach my bedroom and bathroom and outside stairs to get in and out of the house. It is not an aging friendly home, and the high altitude, coupled with long winters and ice on the sidewalks, is not a senior haven of safety or practicality.

Currently, I am very fit and healthy. I swim, dance, ski, hike, play tennis, practice yoga, and walk all over town. However, if an orthopedic degeneration or injury occurred, my stairs would be most inconvenient, potentially painful, and unsafe. If I have an illness or other medical condition, I might need treatment in Denver, a city with more medical resources than a small town offers. As a result of these considerations, I began to see a need for a small residence in Denver. The city is at a lower altitude as well. I also have a social network in Denver. Friends have always been important to me, but they are even more so as I age.

I found and purchased a one-bedroom condo with 821 square feet and a parking spot in a covered garage. Even though for a period of time I will have two residences, I am progressively dropping from 5,567 to 1,836 to 821 square feet! I am still moving in the minimizing direction. My mountain home could be sold or rented out for income as wanted or needed. In my elder years, I could downsize further by moving into a senior housing building or assisted living facility. That move would be less daunting, due to my progressive reduction of space and belongings.

But … you may say that you are full of life and not ready for such thoughts or actions. I, too, am full of life and have definitely not thrown in the towel and given up on living. Minimizing has brought me more energy and freedom than I had when I was weighed down with a large quantity of things and a big house. I can travel more easily and feel less anxiety and stress. I feel satisfaction in handling these matters now instead of delaying them until some sort of crisis occurs that might force a change.

But … you may say you love your stuff. You have valuable collections and are still collecting. I am not suggesting you throw out or give away things of meaning to you. If your tastes have changed, items you used to collect may no longer be important to you. However, someone else might treasure them now.

But … you may say I am morbid for taking such dramatic steps when I am still relatively young. I say I am realistic. Dealing directly with the realities of my aging parents and eldercare smacked me in the face. But instead of feeling defeated by the prospect of ultimately slowing down, I feel lighter and experience more vitality since I let go of unappreciated and unused things in my life. Minimizing can be exhilarating. If you continue decluttering, you just might find a zest for life that you didn't know existed under all that stuff!

Creating an Intentional Living Space

As I downsized progressively, I had the perfect opportunity to create a peaceful haven in my home. When I entered my space, I wanted it to refresh me and feel like a refuge. I wanted a place where I could age gracefully without worrying about stairs or too many things to take care of, dust, and clean. I wanted to be able to "lock and leave" while I traveled. I cut my expenses on unnecessary amenities, services, and maintenance issues. I found a condominium complex where the majority of the residents were downsizing, empty nesters such as myself, so that I had a built-in social network and neighborly support around me. My building is also in walking distance to a light rail station, restaurants, open space, and walking and biking trails.

Viewing Pinterest boards on simple living and visiting stores like IKEA showed me samples of decorating and living efficiently in small spaces, including utilizing multi-functional furniture. As I moved into my new space, I asked myself how I wanted to feel in each room and what its purpose was. My bedroom, for example, is strictly for rest, sleep, replenishment, and intimacy, if I have a partner. It contains no office or exercise equipment, and it is almost free of any electronics except a clock radio, which I have had since the 1970s, when I was a teen!

I have an open floor plan with a large room that contains a kitchen, dining table, and living room space. I also have a study where I placed a small desk. I have a clothes closet, a coat/linen closet, and one bathroom. The few overnight guests I have will sleep on the pullout bed contained within the living room couch. Each item I own has its zone and place where I can easily find it. Entryways and passageways are tidy and unobstructed for good energy flow. My most precious and treasured things are placed where I can gaze at them. My favorite art adorns the walls.

The unit has a small storage cage in the garage area of the building in which I keep my (pared down) favorite holiday decorations. And I bought a used bicycle. When I moved from a three-car garage to no garage, my bicycle was the only thing I missed. So, I allowed myself to purchase a new (to me) used bike.

My smaller living space also made it easier for me to see when clutter might begin to creep in. Peter Walsh suggests these golden rules: "If you get it out—put it away. If you open it—close it. If you finish it—replace it. If it's full—empty it. If you take it off—hang it up. If it's dirty—wash it. If it's garbage—trash it."

In the book *Breathing Room*, the authors talk about passing your stuff through three gates:

Is it true to my intentions?
Do I use it?
Is it kind to my heart and spirit?

When I passed all my things through those gates, here is what I had left:

I use it, and it serves a purpose.
I love to look at it.
I treasure it.
It evokes good feelings.
It aligns with my life now.
It honors parts of my past and family history that I wish to pass down.
It inspires my future and my hopes and dreams.
It creates a positive legacy for my family and not a burden.

Whether you downsize or not, you can still pass your things through gates or tests of your choosing. The end result might just be an oasis that you love to live and unwind in. Create your home to be a place to breathe. We could all use a sanctuary of serenity to deal with the stresses of life.

When You Live with Someone Else

Decluttering can become complicated when you live with another person. Be respectful, and do not throw out the possessions of the person you live with without their permission. It is best to avoid their things completely at first. Most likely, you will be observed as you tidy up. Furthermore, your cleaning efforts might be contagious. Your clearing may inspire those who watch your progress. Over time, your partner or roommate may work together with you, but it is best to concentrate on your own stuff first.

You may need to delineate separate personal space for each person and refrain from placing items in that zone. Perhaps you establish a reading corner, hobby room, or man cave. Each person may work or play there, and it is their business how they decorate or how messy or tidy they keep it. We may not always like or appreciate other people's stuff, but it is important to respect and accept people and their possessions. Our values and priorities might differ. In relationships, we may need to compromise on some points.

Agreements can be made to help maintain harmony. For example, I appreciate returning home to a tidy kitchen and sink. I clean up that area and ask those living with me to do the same after cooking and eating a meal. I make my bed each morning, too, because if I come home to a mess, I feel irritated. I would rather return home and feel the pleasure of entering a peaceful haven.

Pets

Having pets may require more room or a yard. You will invariably have pet stuff: beds, toys, and other parapher-nalia. Financially, you will have food and vet bills. But the benefit of companionship may be worth it to you. For oth-ers, pets can complicate a simplified lifestyle—making it harder, for example, to leave on vacations because you have to find pet care. There are many pros and cons to pet ownership. It is a big responsibility and should be well thought-out.

I had cats and dogs or combinations thereof for thirty consecutive years. When my dog died in 2018, I decided to rest a bit. But I suspect I will have a cat again in my future and even kept two cat bowls that I intend to use. I want to travel a lot at this point in my life, and I have decided to wait a while before I add a furry companion back into my home because it feels unkind to leave it alone while I am on a trip. Finding pet care can be challenging as well. But even though animals add a few extra things in the home, they can also add a lot of love. Limiting the number of pet toys and vacuuming more often may be advisable to maintain a tidy home with a pet.

Aging in Place

As a former physical therapist, I am particularly attuned to ways we might stumble and injure ourselves. For example, I am not a fan of stairs for seniors because I think the fall risk outweighs the fitness gained by using them. Furthermore, stairs can become physically impossible if one has an orthopedic injury, disability, or illness that makes them too strenuous to ascend or descend. Stairs have the potential to be a barrier and confine someone to one part of the house. If you have a goal of aging in place and staying in your home in elder years, it behooves you to analyze your home for obstacles that might hinder functionality.

Many baby boomers are thoroughly unprepared for their own aging and dying unless they, too, have been immersed in eldercare for a parent. I was the primary care manager for each of my parents, which exposed me to a glimpse of my own senior years. Both of my parents were able to remain in their homes until their late eighties. Ultimately, they needed more care than I was able to provide and had to move to a care facility. Ideally, we can simultaneously get ahead of obstacles that might hamper the length of our independence and also be open to moving when we need more care.

Decluttering and downsizing before I am forced to do so also means my kids will have less work and stress when I reach old age or suffer an infirmity. We never know when something will suddenly change. Any of us could receive a diagnosis of an incurable illness, have an accident, need a surgery, become disabled, or develop dementia. In the meantime, while I'm still healthy and mobile, I can play and travel more because I can lock and leave my home. I can set off on adventures because I have freed up money to do so and have less to manage.

Energy

Most people seem to experience a gradual decline in energy as they age. Perhaps they go to bed earlier or sleep less soundly. Stamina during exercise can diminish, and recovery from illness and injury takes longer. Mentally, people also report being more forgetful or a bit scattered.

Oxford Academic's *The Journals of Gerontology* published a report in May 2014 titled *The Material Convoy After Age 50*. The report found: "After age fifty, people are progressively less likely to divest themselves of belongings. After age seventy, about 30 percent of persons say that they have done nothing in the past year to clean out, give away, or donate things, and over 80 percent have sold nothing." The study authors hypothesize that "a major reason for less possession management is the rising risk of poor health at older ages that can limit the capacity to carry out the cognitive, physical, social, and emotional tasks of divestment."

Neither the study authors nor I suggest a correct size for your dwelling or how much stuff is acceptable to keep. "The optimal amount, quantity, volume, or store of possessions in later life is difficult to prescribe; one person's clutter is another person's comfort … One's belongings can be a resource, achievement, and delight, but they may also, by turns, be a burden."

Could clearing clutter help offset the trend of less energy as one ages? American journalist, essayist, and author Katy Butler notes: "As energy becomes a precious and limited resource, simplifying is a survival skill … Moving to a smaller house, reducing the size of a lawn and the number of mutual fund accounts, putting bills on autopay, and decluttering possessions can help you stay independent longer."

Spirituality

Others have eloquently written about the connection of clutter and spirituality. In the book, *Breathing Room: Open Your Heart by Decluttering Your Home* by Lauren Rosenfeld and Dr. Melva Green, the authors address clutter and spirituality. "All clutter affects you spiritually, whether it's home clutter, heart clutter, time clutter, or relationship clutter. It blocks your essential light and your ability to touch the world with that light."

Kim Wolinski, known as "Dr. DeClutter" wrote in *Bella Spark*: "When your life is free of clutter, it becomes much easier to fully experience and appreciate such spiritual qualities as: peace of mind, intuition, inner wisdom, gratitude and appreciation, joy, stillness, being in service, being fully conscious, open to receiving guidance from a Higher Source, living with compassion and generosity, and experiencing the ordinary as extraordinary. When chaos and clutter—inside and out—pull you off center, these spiritual qualities can be blocked from expressing through you."

It is not in the scope of this book to dive deeply into spirituality. However, I want to touch upon the concept. Since I have experienced decluttering and downsizing, I have undergone personal growth and healing as a benefit. I feel more connection to a Higher Power, something larger than myself. Perhaps having less stuff and being less busy has allowed me time to contemplate spiritual matters. This may or may not be an objective for you.

I believe that all change begins within us first. Gandhi echoed that belief when he said, "Be the change you want to see in the world." If we want more healing and peace in the world, let us each start with our homes, our relationships, our mindsets, and ourselves.

One of my favorite spiritual books is *Letting Go: The Pathway of Surrender* by David R. Hawkins, MD, PhD. Hawkins states, "Letting go is one of the most efficacious tools by which to reach spiritual goals." The author talks about the mechanism of letting go, which "involves being aware of a feeling, letting it come up, staying with it, and letting it run its course without wanting to make it different or do anything about it. It means simply to let the feeling be there and to focus on letting out the energy behind it."

Hawkins presents a map of consciousness. For simplicity, I will summarize the scale from his book. He describes the lowest level as being out of the zone, being stuck in negative emotions. From the bottom up: shame, guilt, apathy, grief, and fear. These states usually produce inertia. Then comes desire, anger, and pride, which usually result in hyperactivity. Moving up into the zone of happy and productive are the levels of courage, trust, optimism, and forgiveness. Rising higher to peak performance without stress is the zone of understanding. Lifting up yet again into synchronicity and extraordinary outcomes are the levels of love, gratitude, and joy. Peace and enlightenment are the final, highest levels.

I cannot do justice to the book and the details of Hawkins's work in a few paragraphs. But I have been able to apply his levels of consciousness to many aspects of my life, including my journey in decreasing the amount of stuff in my life, and I encourage you to read his book. For most of my life, I had more physical objects than I needed. Perhaps I still own more things than necessary, but I am moving away from gathering more and am releasing steadily. And it feels good.

Since physical, mental, emotional, and spiritual aspects of life are intertwined, my world has changed in all areas with decluttering and downsizing. If I won the lottery, I doubt I would buy a bigger home and fill it up. I suspect I would invest in experiences and travel and save for my elder years. I would give more to my favorite organizations and causes. Even without a large financial windfall such as a lottery win, I still direct my money toward those ends.

One can certainly be a spiritual or religious person with an untidy or cluttered home. But lying within the declutter journey is the potential to connect with the Divine or deepening that connection. I believe it is there for anyone who seeks it and is open to it. That declaration isn't meant to imply you will become a spiritual guru or an enlightened being by removing clutter in your home. But perhaps you will feel more purpose and meaning in your day-to-day life. Maybe your relationships will deepen. Overwhelm may lessen. Calm focus may be a by-product of clearing. If you decide to embark upon this path of spiritual exploration, may you discover benefits and find blessings along the way. I continue to learn and grow and discoveries are still unfolding.

Unfinished Business

Clearing clutter is much more than cleaning out a closet crammed with things or getting rid of the contents of boxes piled in your basement, attic, or storage unit. Most of us have unfinished business that might feel like we walk around dragging a heavy ball with a chain connected to our ankle. As you declutter and possibly downsize, you have the opportunity to address weighty matters that tie you down physically, mentally, emotionally, and spiritually.

Here are a few ideas to review as we wrap up our time together:

- *Regrets*—is there anything that you can do to address and reduce them?
- *Forgiveness*—is there anyone you need to forgive?
- *Desire to be remembered*—can you create a photo album, scrapbook, video, or memoir?
- *Wish for meaning and purpose*—can you become involved, be an advocate, support a cause, or complete a project that feels purposeful and meaningful to you?

- *Legacy*—can you take steps to provide a positive legacy within your family or community?
- *Giving back*—are there measures you can take to shift toward giving and generosity?
- *Fear and peace of mind*—can you do something now that might reduce your fear and promote ease for yourself and those closest to you?
- *Thankfulness*—is there anyone to whom you can express appreciation and gratitude?
- *Love*—is there someone to whom you might say or write: "I love you"?

This Book Was Originally a Mess

I started writing this book in the summer of 2017. But life got in the way when my mom fell and broke her hip in August of that year. After her hospitalization and rehabilitation stays, I became her full-time caregiver for three months, until the end of 2017. At that point, we decided that the time had arrived for my mom to move to an assisted living facility.

The first four months of 2018 involved that transition, as well as selling my mom's house and dispersing all her possessions that were not moved to her apartment. After her house was sold and she was settled, I visited her weekly and managed her affairs.

I didn't touch the file of this book until January of 2019, after a year and a half of neglect. I also had a notebook filled with scribbled thoughts and scraps of paper that I had added with random ideas to consider. I also had a pile of books that I needed to review and blog posts and articles that needed to be integrated.

Often life slaps us in the face with an unexpected event that derails our plans. Perhaps you can relate to an interrupted project that is incomplete and nearly forgotten. Or maybe you lost your momentum of decluttering your home due to something that sidetracked you. Getting started again can be tough. You may also say you are too busy. I definitely used that excuse for a while.

To bring the chaos of the ideas for this book into an organized form, I had to carve out time from my schedule. I could not accept every invitation that came my way. I had to say no a lot. I became a hermit by day and missed a lot of ski days in the winter of 2019. When I reentered my creative production period of writing, I went into what I call my "monk mode." I was not as social. I got really focused. And for me, a brief time of isolation was worth it. I feel great satisfaction when gathering knowledge and experience and weaving it into a complete, published book.

I also had to allot time for decluttering. Would I have rather been doing something else besides cleaning out closets and basements and boxes? You bet! But again, the end result was worth it to me. We all have a million things vying for our attention. If you tell yourself that you don't have enough time to clear out your junk, you might be delaying the well-being and relief you could experience by tackling it. If not now, when?

Wrapping Up

I am acutely aware of the state of my house and my affairs and how it will affect my daughters when I am no longer living. We leave a legacy behind when we pass, and our stuff is part of that legacy. From "Decluttering as Spiritual Practice" by Lauren Rosenfeld: "Someday, we'll all depart from this world, and we'll all leave behind some of our belongings. We'll want to leave behind things that speak to the life we led. If we declutter, we won't leave people in confusion, wondering what was important to us; it will be made clear by those items we chose to keep in our lives. And remember this: a few boxes of beautifully curated objects is a gift to our loved ones. An attic full of stuff we were afraid to sort through becomes a burden. Start sorting now so you live with only what you love, and what you love is what you'll leave."

Perhaps I always will be in the process of decluttering because things seem to creep in like dust appearing on surfaces. I am getting better at declining free stuff and super cheap or bargain items. Just because it doesn't cost much or is a giveaway doesn't mean it will bring value to my home or my life. I am practicing enjoying things without owning them. I use the library, as well as borrow or rent things that I only need for a short period of time. I also keep digging deeper into the nooks and crannies of my home and uncovering areas that somehow I missed during previous clearing sessions. Occasionally, I find something and say to myself, "Wow, I forgot I had that!" I grin and realize that my own home can still harbor pockets of stuff that escaped my fastidiousness during earlier decluttering periods.

For me, decluttering and downsizing has caused shifts in my thinking and my habits. I don't *have* to declutter; I *choose* to declutter. I have detached my self-worth from the size of my home and love the coziness of my new, smaller space. Designing a new living arrangement provided me with a fresh start. I realize that not all my stuff is important, and I like having fewer things that matter the most to me. Instead of getting pleasure from buying things, I now find enjoyment in rehoming stuff I don't use or like anymore. Instead of thinking I am losing something when I clear clutter, I dwell on what I might gain. I have listened to the stories behind the stuff I held onto, and I processed my past while releasing it. I then moved into a vibrant present and hopeful future. I redirected my money from purchasing and collecting trivial items toward more meaningful endeavors.

For me, decluttering and downsizing has brought me more freedom. Francine Jays echoes that feeling: "With minimalist living comes freedom—freedom from debt, from clutter, and from the rat race. Each extraneous thing you eliminate from your life feels like a weight lifted from your shoulders. You'll have fewer errands to run and less to shop for, pay for, clean, maintain, and insure. Moreover, when you're not chasing status symbols or keeping up with the Joneses, you gain time and energy for more ful-filling pursuits: like playing with your kids, participating in your community, and pondering the meaning of life." And for those who are older, it may be grandkids who get more of your time and energy.

A Millennial Perspective

I was born at the end of the baby boomer generation, and my two daughters are in their mid-twenties and in the millennial generation. My oldest daughter, thirty years younger than me, shared her thoughts on minimalism.

I think the main thing that is different about mini-malism for me compared to my mom's generation is that minimalism doesn't feel like some new or crazy concept to try out—it's more like common sense. I think that is why I am less interested in reading or learning more about it because I feel like it's something that's almost subconsciously wired into me. I don't think this is necessarily the same for everyone in my generation though. For being pretty young, I have moved a lot of places and traveled a lot, so minimalism is something that came about for me for practical reasons.

I also have chosen to pursue a line of work that is more about feeling a sense of purpose every day versus making money and chasing success. On top of my already minimalist tendencies from traveling so much, working as a social worker has pushed me into an even more extreme form of minimalism. I am very aware of what in my life constitutes a luxury versus a necessity. If anything, I am trying to include more luxuries in my life and allow myself to spend money now on things that bring me joy, whereas before I would only permit myself the necessities. So I am actually backing off a little from my hard-core minimalism and seeking a balance.

However, even if I were to make boatloads of money someday, minimalism is something so deeply wired within me that I don't know that I would care to change much of my external circumstances. Sure, I would love to have a home of my own and to be able to travel more, but there aren't that many possessions that I long for or crave. To me, possessions often end up feeling more like a burden than anything else. I love the ability to move about freely and travel lightly, and too many possessions can be a huge hindrance to this lifestyle. My thoughts can be summarized with the expression: "What you own owns you."

As far as observing my mom's struggles clearing my grandparents' homes, owning and remaining attached to a large amount of possessions is something almost mind-boggling to me. I just don't get it. That being said, I do have compassion for the fact that my grandparents grew up in the Great Depression and were raised in an era when every item was reused and repurposed out of practicality; hardly anything was thrown away.

Regarding my generation as a whole: I think that there is a split happening. On one hand, there are the people, like my friends and me, who live simple, value-based, minimalist lives and cherish experiences over possessions. This group within my generation is into mindfulness practices. They are often vegan—or at least very conscious of their health. Many of them are artists or healers as well. They love to travel, so much so that many of them are willing to live in their cars or their RVs. This group prioritizes community and relationships. They think deeply about consumerism and how their actions affect the world.

There is also another group within my generation, which I think of as "the people who bought into the ads." This group spends most of their days staring at screens. By spending so much time on social media, it is all too easy to fall into the trap of comparing yourself with the pictures of the people around you. Because of these comparisons, this group cultivates and cares a lot about the image they broadcast of themselves. They often get fooled into believing that this image is who they really are. They tend to shop compulsively, watch a lot of TV, eat out frequently, and spend a good chunk of their paychecks on going out on the weekends and partying. They wear their worth on their bodies in the form of new clothes, gear, and gadgets.

It's hard to tell which of these two groups is larger or which will "win out" in the end, in terms of influence. The two groups do interact and influence each other in sometimes subtle ways, so there can be a good amount of crossover between these seemingly separate groups.

—Summer

My youngest daughter, thirty-one years younger than me, also shared her thoughts.

My relationship with stuff has evolved over time. At first, I very much prioritized and protected the material things in my life, but my stance has relaxed on it quite a bit in recent years. As a younger person, I had a preoccupation with caring for, maintaining, and protecting my things because they offered me security and luxury. It was never the money or the status that attracted me, it was always the safety and leverage I felt from being "well-surrounded" in such a dense and physical world. I prided myself on my ability to care for my things, while it seemed like so many of my peers were so reckless with their stuff. I would notice it would tend to catch up with them later because they would have to buy new belongings after losing the original ones.

However, gradually I became aware that my fierce and natural propensity to guard my items also led to a lot of energy spent staying vigilant, wary, and "clutching tightly." It also seemed that it would alienate others, and some would criticize and judge me for the trait. Over time, I would start to experiment with the choice of selling or giving away some of my belongings, and I would notice energy opening up to be used in more conscientious, creative, and charitable ways. I then took it a step further and tried to relax my grip a bit on the items I had left by letting others borrow my things. I also relaxed and cared less if the wear and tear of life started to make its inevitable mark on my stuff.

I decided to sell my car in 2018. This decision was sparked from an inner desire to reduce the stress that comes with owning a car: the payments, the gas, the maintenance, the parking, the driving, the sitting, the contribution to the petroleum business, and environmental degradation. Doing research on other people who had gone car-free was a huge inspiration for me, as I had read that the liberation that followed was almost always worth the extra effort to find other means of transportation.

From the moment that car title was transferred, I felt immediate relief and continue to feel a deep sense of ease from not having the responsibility tugging at me. The only main potential downside is the decrease in convenience, but I personally don't mind and even mostly enjoy taking public transportation, walking, riding my bike in the fresh air, or sharing a ride with a friend or family member. It's led to a greater quality of life for me. I am also conscious of contributing and finding win-wins, so as to not feel like I'm mooching off of other people's resources. Overall, it was one of the best decisions I've made for this period of my life, and quite frankly, I don't really miss it one bit. But I also acknowledge that for some people and for some times of life, a car can open many doors that would not otherwise be opened. I think it depends on the person, the environment in which we live, and our resources and goals.

I have learned a lot just by witnessing my mom's struggles with clearing her own home and those of her parents. It left its mark and impression on me. I am often floored when I observe the accumulation that other people have amassed and am amazed that they are able to continue on with life in such a way that to me feels very heavy and tied down. I so value the freedom and lightness that comes with owning fewer things, and it's a stretch for me to place myself into the shoes of others who prioritize the other end of the spectrum. But as far as my grandparents, there isn't much room to be harsh on them because they grew up in a different time.

With my millennial peers, I am more among what is portrayed as the "norm" in the media, if not even swaying a little more toward holding onto and revering possessions. My peers are big into being a generation of "digital nomads" and minimalists—many are choosing not to buy homes or cars, opting for subscription meal plans delivered to their doors and preferring a digital dating experience—a generation living a lifestyle where work, residence, transportation, nutrition, and relationships promote freedom as much as possible. Many of this, but not all, I resonate with, and of course, with any lifestyle comes certain blindsides. For millennials, this might be flightiness, impatience, and a hesitancy to commit.

Generally, I am excited for the future we are heading toward, all the while aiming to weigh the importance of many different ways of life and perspectives. It often feels like generations are waves of similar-minded people with a lot of new perspectives and styles to offer to the world, and more often than not, I am excited to be a part of that.

—Liberty

"I want to shed my waste
with quiet reverence like the pine …
Keep me mindful of what I take into my home,
the items bought to substitute for real living …
Help me slowly to surrender all excess."
—Gunilla Norris, *Being Home*

Feedback

Thank you for spending time with me. If you kept highlights or notes, let me know what sections spoke to you or inspired action. What reasons for decluttering and downsizing were most compelling to you? What benefits did you experience?

Reach out to me on my website www.LisaJShultz.com and share your takeaways. If you have a success story, I may feature it on my blog with your permission. Before and after pictures are not required, but I love them!

Please write a book review on a purchase platform or Goodreads, including what aspect of my book had the most positive impact for you. This detail helps potential readers know if the book might be helpful to them.

Endnotes, Books, Blogs, and Websites

*Note: I often reference an author or site more than once in my book. I acknowledge the reference here in the first place it appears. I thank each contributor who influenced me and hope my readers might find some of these resources helpful.

Introduction

Who Am I and Where Did I Start?

Ashi. 2009. *Bless Your Mess and Create a Home That Feels Fabulous!: A Guide to Clutter-Free Living*. Denver, CO: Cedar Rose Press.

2014. "For Many People, Gathering Possessions Is Just the Stuff of Life." *Los Angeles Times*. March 21, 2014. https://www.latimes.com/health/la-xpm-2014-mar-21-la-he-keeping-stuff-20140322-story.html.

Is This Book About Minimalism?

Heisler, Yoni, and Yoni Heisler. 2009. "Steve Jobs in His Living Room, circa 1982." Network World. April 16, 2009. https://www.networkworld.com/article/2235320/steve-jobs-in-his-living-room-circa-1982.html.

Sasaki, Fumio. 2017. *Goodbye, Things: The New Japanese Minimalism*. New York: W.W. Norton & Company.

Becker, Joshua. n.d. "Becoming Minimalist." Accessed August 13, 2019. https://www.becomingminimalist.com/.

2019. "Ma (Negative Space)." Wikimedia Foundation. August 2, 2019. https://en.m.wikipedia.org/wiki/Ma_(negative_space).

Brownell, Lauren Cassel. 2008. *Zen and the Art of Housekeeping: The Path to Finding Meaning in Your Cleaning*. Avon, MA: Adams Media.

Additional Support

"Hips Don't Lie: Releasing Old Emotions Through Hip Openers." YogaToday.com. Accessed August 13, 2019. https://www.yogatoday.com/blog/hips-dont-lie-releasing-stored-up-emotion-through-hip-openers.

"Meetings." Clutterers Anonymous. Accessed August 13, 2019. https://clutterersanonymous.org/meetings/.

Building a Case for Decluttering and Downsizing

Walsh, Peter. 2009. *It's All Too Much: Workbook: The Tools You Need to Conquer Clutter and Create the Life You Want.* New York: Free Press.

Magnusson, Margareta. 2019. *The Gentle Art of Swedish Death Cleaning.* Leicester: Thorpe, Isis.

Family Chaos

Hall, Julie. 2008. *The Boomer Burden: Dealing with Your Parents Lifetime Accumulation of Stuff.* Nashville: Thomas Nelson.

Sudden Death

D'Argonne, Sawyer. 2018. "Family Remembers Arvada Man Who Died Following Cardiac Event at Keystone Resort." SummitDaily.com. December 29, 2018. https://www.summitdaily.com/news/family-remembers-arvada-man-who-died-following-cardiac-event-at-keystone-resort/.

McKeown, Greg. 2014. *Essentialism: The Disciplined Pursuit of Less*. London: Virgin Books.

What is the Point of Decluttering My Life?

Carver, Courtney. 2017. *Soulful Simplicity: How Living with Less Can Lead to so Much More*. NY, NY: Penguin Random House.

Rosenfeld, Lauren, and Melva Green. 2014. *Breathing Room: Open Your Heart by Decluttering Your Home*. London: Atria.

Alan Arkin, *Out of My Mind* (Audible, 2017).

Jay, Francine. 2016. *The Joy of Less: A Minimalist Guide to Declutter, Organize, and Simplify*. San Francisco: Chronicle Books.

Digging In and Digging Out

Schedule It

Covey, Stephen R. 2004. *The 7 Habits of Highly Effective People*. London: Pocket Books.

Hold It in Your Hands

Kondo, Marie, and Cathy Hirano. 2017. *Spark Joy*. London: Vermilion.

Clothes

"Project 333." n.d. Be More with Less. Accessed August 16, 2019. https://bemorewithless.com/project-333/.

Bloem, Craig. 2018. "Why Successful People Wear the Same Thing Every Day." Inc.com. February 20, 2018. https://www.inc.com/craig-bloem/this-1-unusual-habit-helped-make-mark-zuckerberg-steve-jobs-dr-dre-successful.html.

Kitchen and Food Waste

2019. "Keep Fruits & Vegetables Fresher for Longer." The Swag. May 9, 2019. https://www.theswag.com.au/.

Gifts

"The Five Love Languages And What They Mean." 2019. Crated With Love. June 24, 2019. https://cratedwithlove.com/blog/five-love-languages-and-what-they-mean/.

Catalogs, Magazines and Books

"Junk Mail Facts and Statistics." n.d. Waste. Accessed August 16, 2019. http://wasteawaygroup.blogspot.com/2018/01/junk-mail-facts-and-statistics.html.

Admin. n.d. "How to Stop Junk Mail." Eco. Accessed August 16, 2019. http://www.ecocycle.org/junkmail.

Enrich or Ditch

Abandoned Hobbies, Sports Equipment, Pet Ashes, and the Potentially Useful

Tatsumi, Nagisa. 2017. *The Art of Discarding: How to Get Rid of Clutter and Find Joy.* New York: Hachette Books.

Heirlooms and Collections

Sall, Lisa Sall. 1970. "Shakespeare Garden." Shakespeare Garden. January 1, 1970. http://shakespearegarden. blogspot.com/.

Massello, Melissa. 2019. "Sorry, Parents: Nobody Wants the Family 'Heirlooms.'" Apartment Therapy. Apartment Therapy, LLC. May 3, 2019. https://www.apartmentther-apy.com/sorry-parents-nobody-wants-the-family-heir-looms-249266.

Additional Considerations

Financial

Ramsey, Dave. 2009. *The Total Money Makeover: A Proven Plan for Financial Fitness.* Nashville, TN: Thomas Nelson Pub.

Social Media, Email and Technology

Carr, Nicholas. 2020. *Shallows: What the Internet Is Doing to Our Brains.* S.L.: W.W. Norton.

Sustainability and Environmental Impact

Legally Sociable. 2011. "Sierra Club Green Home Member Suggests 1,000 per Person in Future Homes." Legally Sociable. June 10, 2011. https://legallysociable.com/2011/06/10/sierra-club-green-home-member-suggests-1000-per-person-in-future-homes/.

Bugbee, Paul. 2017. "The American Dream? Check the Landfill." *St. Cloud Times*. September 21, 2017. https://www.sctimes.com/story/opinion/2017/09/21/american-dream-check-landfill/680301001/.

Amadeo, Kimberly. 2019. "3 Reasons Why Americans Are in So Much Debt." The Balance. July 8, 2019. https://www.thebalance.com/consumer-debt-statistics-causes-and-impact-3305704.

"Green Generation: Millennials Say Sustainability Is a Shopping Priority." Nielsen. May 11, 2015. http://www.nielsen.com/us/en/insights/news/2015/green-generation-millennials-say-sustainability-is-a-shopping-priority.html.

Carbon Footprint

"Carbon Footprint." 2019. Wikipedia. Wikimedia Foundation. August 15, 2019. https://en.wikipedia.org/wiki/Carbon_footprint.

"Top 20 Ways to Reduce Your Carbon Footprint." n.d. Accessed August 17, 2019. http://www.globalstewards.org/reduce-carbon-footprint.htm.

Holth, Jesse. 2017. "7 Instant Ways To Reduce Your Carbon Footprint." *The Huffington Post*. 6, 2017. https://www.huffingtonpost.com/entry/7-instant-ways-to-reduce-your-carbon-footprint_us_59321992e4b00573ab57a383.

Health

Beau, Emilie Le. 2019. "The Unbearable Heaviness of Clutter." *The New York Times*. January 3, 2019. https://www.nytimes.com/2019/01/03/well/mind/clutter-stress-procrastination-psychology.html.

"Cortisol: What It Does & How To Regulate Cortisol Levels." n.d. WebMD. WebMD. Accessed August 17, 2019. https://www.webmd.com/a-to-z-guides/what-is-cortisol#1.

Hay, Louise L., and Susan Gross. 2009. *Heal Your Body A-Z: The Mental Causes for Physical Illness and the Way to Overcome Them*. Carlsbad (California): Hay House.

The Antiaging Movement

Furstenberg, Diane Von. 2015. *The Woman I Wanted to Be*. New York: Simon & Schuster.

Feng Shui

Kingston, Karen. 2017. *Clear Your Clutter with Feng Shui*. London: Piatkus.

Lifelong Decluttering and Simplifying

Energy

J., David, Baker, and Lindsey A. 2014. "Material Convoy After Age 50." OUP Academic. *Oxford University Press.* February 11, 2014. https://academic.oup.com/psych-socgerontology/article/69/3/442/625042.

Butler, Katy. 2020. *Art of Dying Well: A Practical Guide to a Good End of Life.* S.L.: Scribner.

Spirituality

Hawkins, David R. 2018. *Letting Go: The Pathway of Surrender.* Carlsbad, CA: Hay House, Inc.

Final Thoughts

Wrapping Up

Rosenfeld, LG. 2015. "Decluttering as Spiritual Practice." Medium. August 14, 2015. https://medium.com/@LGRosenfeld/decluttering-as-a-spiritual-practice-c5be-27485dee.

Feedback

Norris, Gunilla, and Greta Sibley. 2001. *Being Home: Discovering the Spiritual in the Everyday.* Mahwah, NJ: Hidden Spring.

Acknowledgments

My parents for their love and generosity.
Siblings for harmony while clearing parental homes.
Bobby Haas for structure and editing.
Andrea Costantine for cover design and layout.
Jenna Zelinger for proofreading.
Polly Letofsky for advice during the publishing process.
Phil Blighton for my author photo.
Staci Shultz for raising the bar to encourage my best
writing with questions and suggestions.
Summer and Liberty for your contribution and beautiful
presence in my life.
Numerous friends for encouragement and support.
Denver Woman's Press Club, fellow authors, and book
lovers for spreading the word about my book to others.

About the Author

Lisa J. Shultz is an award winning author and baby boomer with a zest for conversation about what matters the most in life and death. She finds herself in midlife writing about a variety of topics that call to her heart. She has moved beyond the stage of actively raising her daughters, but she enjoys their visits and learns from their millennial views. Colorado is her home state, but she also loves to travel, which widens her awareness to our connectedness and also differing regional and cultural perspectives.

Lisa offers consultation and coaching for those who desire support and accountability with decluttering goals. She is also available to speak to groups and enjoys visiting book clubs.

Her previous book, *A Chance to Say Goodbye: Reflections on Losing a Parent*, explores her relationship with her father and the end of his life. She wrote it to guide and support those facing the loss of a parent or healing from that loss.

For more information on books she has written or services she offers, visit her website: www.LisaJShultz.com

Manufactured by Amazon.ca
Bolton, ON

27015093R00085